Finding Peace in Your Pain

Life Lessons from the Story of Job

Dr. David O. Dykes

Author of Handling Life's Disappointments

For Lizzie and Caroline,
my two granddaughters.
You put a smile on my face
and hope in my heart.

Also by David O. Dykes

Do Angels Really Exist? Separating Fact from Fantasy

Handling Life's Disappointments:
   Moving from Desperation to Celebration

Character out of Chaos:
   Daring to be a Daniel in Today's World

Ten Requirements for America's Survival

Angels Really Do Exist: Signs of Heaven on Earth

Table of Contents

INTRODUCTION

If you're searching for easy answers and quick fixes for your pain, this book isn't for you. Put it back on the shelf and look elsewhere. I wrote this book for people who are hurting and whose eyes brim over with tears at the least provocation. It doesn't contain advice on seven things to do to mend your heart by next Tuesday. At first, you may think that this book contains more questions than answers. In fact, you'll soon discover that the book of Job contains more questions than any book in the Bible, and the vast majority of those questions are left unanswered. God Himself steps into the story and asks questions that are far beyond our ability to comprehend, much less answer!

Even people unfamiliar with the Bible can usually recall a portion of the plot of Job's story. How many times have you heard people say to someone going through a struggle, "You must have the patience of Job"? Suffering and heartache are inextricably attached to Job's name. Although it's one of the oldest stories in all of literature, Job's story never goes out of vogue for one undeniable reason: we have to deal with pain and suffering. Job said it well when he lamented, "Yet man is born to trouble as surely as sparks fly upward" Job 5:7.

You've probably discovered that your Creator designed you with the peculiar ability to produce moisture from your eyes whenever you cry—tears. I considered naming this book, "Turning Tears into Telescopes" because Job teaches how our tears help us see into heaven, much like a telescope helps us gaze into the starry skies. Through the lens of a telescope, it's possible to see things never seen with the naked eye. Likewise, looking through your teardrops can enable you to gaze into the face of God and see that you are deeply loved—even when you aren't feeling very loved. Childlike trust allows you to be embraced by God's amazing grace—even when you aren't feeling grace-full. When your heart is breaking and your eyes fill with tears, it's easy for you to ask God to change your situation. However, God is often more interested in changing *you* rather than changing your painful situation.

One of my mentors, Ron Dunn, used to say that the spiritual life of most Christians can be compared to his grandmother's old feather bed: firm on both ends and sagging in the middle! In other words, most of us are firm in our belief that we once trusted Christ for salvation (our conversion experience). And we are rock solid in our belief that one day in the future we'll be with Jesus in heaven. However, it's the middle experience that we call daily life where we're sagging sometimes. Those who only relate to the first and last chapters of Job are "sagging in the middle"! In the first chapter, Job loses it all; in the last chapter, he gets it all back again (with heavenly compound interest). As the book ends, Job lives happily ever after. Right?

Wait a minute. That's not the full story. That truncated glimpse misses the point and robs the story of its significance. Only in the "middle chapters" can you see how frustrating life can be. Most of us spend our days in those messy middle chapters of Job and will only arrive at the "happily ever after" when we pass on into the arms of Jesus.

However, lest you find yourself sagging even deeper into despair, stop your pity party right there! The wonderful message of the Bible (and that includes Job) is that there is *always hope*. I believe the four letters in the word "hope" stand for Having Only Positive Expectations! If, like Isaiah's description of the Messiah, you find yourself facing sorrow and you are acquainted with grief, prepare to be encouraged. If you'll immerse yourself in the truths hidden just below the surface within the story of Job, you can certainly find God's peace in your pain.

Three decades ago, I heard a poem that so impressed me that I memorized it on the spot. Although I've never discovered the author, I've never forgotten it. It expresses what I hope you'll experience as we begin our journey through Job's story:

I walked a mile with laughter,
She chatted all the way.
But I was none the wiser,
For all she had to say.

I walked a mile with sorrow,
And not a word said she.
But, oh, the things I learned,
When sorrow walked with me!

-Anonymous

"The truth that many people never understand, until it is too late, is that the more you try to avoid suffering the more you suffer because smaller and more insignificant things begin to torture you in proportion to your fear of being hurt."

–Thomas Merton

CHAPTER 1

The Peril of
Fair-Weather Faith

Her name was Jeannette Davis, and since I was in my mid-twenties, she seemed ancient at age 35. She and her husband, Ray, were members of the little church in Central Alabama that had been brave enough to hire a rookie pastor like me. Ray attended church faithfully, but Jeanette? Never. Actually, she seldom moved far from her couch. She suffered from a severe case of rheumatoid arthritis. I can't erase the memory of the first time I visited her at home. The arthritis had reshaped her skeleton into a collection of odd angles. Yet her smile was straight and strong as she held out her drawn and bent fingers to shake my hand. I took her hand lightly, thinking I might cause her pain, only to be surprised by the strength of her grip. Her eyes were clear as we spoke about the things most people like to talk about with pastors: her family, faith, and health.

As I prepared to leave, she asked if I would pray for her, which I gladly did. Before I could open my eyes after my "amen" she began to pray an unforgettable prayer. It was the prayer of a person who is intimate with the Almighty. I don't recall much of her words because I lost it when she prayed, "Dear God, thank you for being so good to me." When she finished her prayer, there were tears in her eyes, and Ray and I were wiping our cheeks as well. In that moment, all my seminary—driven motivation to be a teacher surrendered to the fact that she was teaching me more truth than I could ever impart to her.

Years later, when I learned that Jeanette had finally escaped her broken body, I wept again, but this time I shed tears of joy. I imagined her ecstasy at being set free to see her Savior without having to gaze through her veil of tears. Job, Jeanette, and the other saints who maintain faith in the midst of pain have something valuable to teach those who tend to flounder amid fair-weather faith. Let's pick up the story of Job at the beginning:

> Job 1:1-12: *In the land of Uz there lived a man whose name was Job. This man was blameless and upright; he feared God and shunned evil. He had seven sons and three daughters, and he owned seven thousand sheep, three thousand camels, five hundred yoke of oxen and five hundred donkeys, and had a large number of servants. He was the greatest man among all the people of the East. His sons used to take turns holding feasts in their homes, and they would invite their three sisters to eat and drink with them. When a period of feasting had run its course, Job would send and have them purified. Early in the morning he would sacrifice a burnt offering for each of them, thinking, "Perhaps my children have sinned and cursed God in their hearts." This was Job's regular custom. One day the angels came to present themselves before the Lord, and Satan also came with them. The Lord said to Satan, "Where have you come from?" Satan answered the Lord, "From roaming through the earth and going back and forth in it." Then the Lord said to Satan, "Have you considered my servant Job? There is no one on earth like him; he is blameless and upright, a man who fears God and shuns evil." "Does Job fear*

2

> *God for nothing?" Satan replied. "Have you*
> *not put a hedge around him and his household*
> *and everything he has? You have blessed the*
> *work of his hands, so that his flocks and herds*
> *are spread throughout the land. But stretch out*
> *your hand and strike everything he has, and he*
> *will surely curse you to your face." The Lord*
> *said to Satan, "Very well, then, everything he*
> *has is in your hands, but on the man himself do*
> *not lay a finger." Then Satan went out from the*
> *presence of the Lord.*

Literary scholars claim that Job is one of the oldest books in history. It is written in poetic form like Psalms, Proverbs, Song of Solomon, Ecclesiastes, and Lamentations. Old Testament experts believe that Job was written as an epic drama, like Homer's *Iliad* and *Odyssey*. However, that's not to suggest that Job was a fictional character. You could write a drama based on the life of George Washington, but that wouldn't make him a fictional character. In the same way, most scholars believe Job was a real person who lived about 2,000 B.C. Even outside its biblical significance, the story of Job is considered to be one of the most profound pieces of literature in all of history. The French writer Victor Hugo wrote: "If all the world's literary efforts were to be destroyed, and I could save but a solitary sample, it would be Job."

Why Do the Righteous Suffer?
Most people are interested in Job because they can relate to the theme of a book that addresses the question: "Why do the righteous suffer?" As I was writing this book, a friend of mine remarked how similar her life is to Job's. She said, "So many things have happened to me that my friends started calling me Job-ette!" Most people, whether they are Job or Job-ette, can relate to suffering.

The first twelve verses in chapter one of Job set the

stage for the entire drama to unfold. In order to understand how the beginning affects Job's entire story, I need to provide a brief synopsis of the book. In 1825, the English poet and artist, William Blake, prepared 21 engravings illustrating the book of Job. In the first scene, Job and his family are gathered together and everything is wonderful. They have each other, good health, and an abundance of wealth. In the next engraved scene, God is on His throne with all the angels (good and bad) gathered around Him. After God's conversation with Satan, the devil sets out to prove that Job only fears God because he has been so blessed. In the next scene, Satan is seen striking Job's children with a catastrophic storm in which all of them perish. In the next scene, Satan attacks Job's health, afflicting him with painful skin sores. All of this occurs in the first two chapters!

In the next scene in the engravings, Job's wife and three friends are pointing their fingers at him as if to taunt him. Most people know the first and last part of the story, but the largest portion of the book is devoted to the rounds of conversation between Job and his friends: Eliphaz, Bildad, and Zophar. These guys believed Job was suffering because he had done something wrong. They tried to persuade him to come clean and reveal his deep dark sin. We'll have much more to say about these "friends" in Chapter 5 entitled, "With Friends Like These, Who Needs Enemies?"

In the climax of the story, God speaks to Job out of a whirlwind. He asks Job, "What makes you think you're smart enough to figure out why I do anything?" In the final scene of the story, Job prays for his friends, and God restores to Job more than he ever had before. When you consider the entire plot of Job's story, you'll see five important insights about finding peace in your pain.

INSIGHT #1: There Is More Going on around You Than You Can See

At the start of the story, Job saw his happy family and all of his possessions before him, but his limited earthly vision prevented him from seeing what was taking place in heaven. He could hear his cattle lowing and his sheep bleating, but he couldn't hear the conversation going on between God and Satan. However, as readers of the book, we can see what is simultaneously happening in heaven.

Chapter 1 says: *One day the angels* ("sons of Elohim") *came to present themselves* ("to stand and report") *before the Lord and Satan* ("the adversary") *also came with them"* (Job 1:6). Who were these "sons of elohim?" Throughout the Old Testament, there are references to other "gods." The Hebrew word for God is "El" and "Elohim" is simply the plural "gods." However, there is only one true Almighty God. His name in Hebrew came from the four consonants YHWH, usually pronounced, "Yahweh." (Yahweh has been "Germanized" and "Anglicized" to become *Jehovah* in English.) A god can be anything or anyone to whom a person gives ultimate allegiance. That's why our God demands, *"You shall have no other gods (elohim) before me"* (Exodus 20:3).

It would be the pinnacle of presumption for us to think that we are the only beings in God's creation. We are human beings, but the Bible teaches that there are innumerable hosts of heavenly beings created by God. These beings are generally called angels, but the Bible indicates there are many kinds of angels or heavenly creatures—good and bad.

Most of us remember the bizarre creatures from the first Star Wars movie when Luke and Obie Wan Kenobie visit a bar in Tatooin. Angels and demons aren't that strange, but when you read the Bible, you discover there is a fantastic variety in God's heavenly beings. For instance, in Revelation 4, there are four "creatures" who worship God continually—the KJV translated the word "beasts." There are seraphim and cherubim as well. This is just another indication that we are surrounded by an entire invisible world, populated by heavenly creatures we cannot observe with our human eyes.

What's Outside the Frame of the Screen?

It's like a movie director investigating a location for a film scene. He puts his hands out with his thumbs together to make a model of a screen. He knows he can put an image in that frame and the audience won't see anything else. When you're watching a movie or a television show, you only see a small slice of reality. The director doesn't want you to see what is outside the frame, like the lights, the studio, the set, or the assistants holding microphones.

Sometimes when you're watching a cheap movie or television show you can see a microphone accidentally slip in from the top of the screen. Or you may catch a glimpse of telephone poles that seem strangely out of place in a western. When you see something like that, it reminds you that what you're seeing is only a sliver of reality. There's more there than meets the eye.

The same is true of this world. The Bible says, *"So we fix our eyes not on what is seen, but on what is unseen. For what is seen is temporary, but what is unseen is eternal"* (2 Corinthians 4:18). We can only see a sliver of reality. An uncanny amount of spiritual warfare and spiritual activity is going on around us "outside the frame" that we cannot see. Occasionally, God allows a spiritual microphone or power line to slip into the screen to remind us that we aren't alone in this world (or the next world). So, whenever you want to pull out your hair and ask, "What in the world is going on?" remember this: it's not what's in *this world* that's going on. It's whatever is happening in *that world* that's really going on!

INSIGHT #2: God Wants to Have a Personal Relationship with You

The current hot scientific debate is between the theories of evolution versus intelligent design (ID). Many Christians are cheering for the ID side of the debate, but some of the proponents of ID often insist that they aren't talking about a personal God. They embrace more of a Deism stance. Deism is the belief that there is some god-like intelligence somewhere, but we aren't privy to any personal information about him/it. In that sense, deism may be a good starting point, but it's a horrible place to finish.

The Bible teaches from the first verse in Genesis that the mighty Creator of the universe wants to have a personal relationship with His creatures. To put it another way, the message of the Bible is not to teach *how* God created the heavens and the earth; instead, it teaches *why* God created the heavens and earth. As the Westminster Catechism suggests, God created you to glorify and enjoy Him forever.

God Knows Your Name

It's important to note that God, not Satan, brings up the subject of Job. He asks Satan, *"Have you considered my servant Job? There is no one on earth like him; he is blameless and upright, a man who fears God and shuns evil"* (Job 1:8). Why would God do that? I believe it was because He loved Job and was proud of Him. It's like when a new grandparent asks you, "Have you seen a picture of my grandchild?" They bring up the topic of their new grandchild for the same reason God was showing off His servant.

God knew Job's name and Job's heart. It can either be comforting or scary to realize that God knows the same things about you that He knew about Job. To our government, you are mainly known by your tax payer identification number, not by your name. However, you're not a number to God. He knows you by name.

Furthermore, God knows your character. God told Satan that Job was "blameless." That doesn't mean perfect; it means he had a good reputation. God boasted, "He is upright." That meant Job was a straight-talking guy. God knew Job's heart better than Job knew himself. God knows everything about you, and He still desires to have a personal relationship with you.

7

INSIGHT #3: Satan Actively Assaults God's Servants
The name "Satan" literally means "adversary." He opposes
God and every potential servant of God. He wants to make your
life miserable. Satan wasn't thinking of Job's well being when
he suggested, *"Stretch out your hand and strike everything he
has, and he will surely curse you to your face"* (Job 1:11).

In a scientific world, many people scoff at the idea of a
devil. However, Satan is not some comic character dressed in
red flannel underwear with two horns, shoveling coal in hell. In
fact, in Job Satan isn't in hell at all. He is roaming throughout
the earth. The Apostle Peter confirmed this when he warned,
*"Your enemy, the devil, prowls around like a roaring lion
looking for someone to devour"* (1 Peter 5:8). Satan is actively,
aggressively, continually working to try to make people curse
God to His face. All you have to do is turn on your televisions,
radios, or surf the internet to confirm that he is finding great
success in America and around the world.

**INSIGHT #4: Genuine Faith in a Loving God Will Sustain
You through Trouble**
The Bible says that when you go through trials and tribulations,
it is a *testing* of your faith. However, contrary to what many
Christians believe, God isn't testing your faith to find out what
kind of faith you possess (as if He doesn't already know). He
already knows everything about you, including the current
quality of your faith. It is very important to understand that the
testing of your faith is to show *you* what kind of faith you have.
The testing of our faith is a self-graded test. You need to know
whether you have a genuine faith because only that kind of faith
will sustain you when you face trouble. As Christians, there are
three different kinds of faith that we tend to demonstrate:

***Fair-Weather Faith: "As long as things are sunny, I'll praise
the Lord!"***
Fair-weather faith operates best when the sun is shining and
life is going our way. Satan accused Job of having this kind

of temperamental faith. In essence the devil told God, "Job is being blessed, but if you take away his blessings, He'll curse you." Satan was wrong about Job, but he was right about many of us—that's the kind of faith we have.

I've observed that some people approach religion like a business deal. They negotiate the terms of their faith just like a business contract. As long as the first party (God) abides with His end of the deal (e.g. blessings, peace, joy), the second party (me) will keep my part of the agreement (e.g. worship, service, offerings). They never say it, of course, but the fair-weather faithful are thinking, "God, if you scratch my back, I'll scratch yours." One immediate problem with that attitude is that God doesn't have a back, and if He did, He would never need us to scratch it!

We've all known people who seem outwardly faithful to God. They attend, give, and serve the Lord in their congregations. However, when they have their feet cut out from under them by a personal crisis, they disappear. It may be a divorce, an illness, or a mean-as-the-devil church member who mistreated them, but when the clouds of adversity gather, they go AWOL from God's army. It's almost as if they decide to boycott God because they think they deserve better treatment.

Foul-Weather Faith: "When the storms of life blow in, I'll call upon the Lord!"

Those who possess this kind of faith are the antithesis of the fair-weather faithful. They say, "When my life is a mess, I'll call upon the Lord!" Before we address this kind of faith, let me assure you that I highly recommend calling on the Lord in times of trouble. The Bible says, *"What time I am afraid, I will trust in you"* (Psalm 56:3). However, the kind of people I'm describing here seem to *only* call upon the Lord when they're afraid and facing a crisis. Once things settle back down to normal, they seem to forget about needing God. God is like that life preserver under your airline seat that says, "For emergency use only." It's been said that "there's no such thing as an atheist

9

in a fox hole." When the bullets are buzzing and the bombs are dropping, some soldiers pray when they would otherwise not call upon the Almighty. Many Christians practice the same fox-hole religion. When the bullets of suffering are buzzing by and the bombs of adversity are falling around us, we become prayer warriors par excellence.

The person with this kind of faith often bargains with God as well. Have you ever prayed a prayer like, "God if you will only help me through this mess, then I'll serve you for the rest of my life!" However, after you survived the crisis you soon forgot your promise? You may not pray another prayer like that until the next crisis arises. Do remember what happened on the Sunday following the 9/11 attacks on the World Trade Center and the Pentagon? Churches were packed with people who feared what might happen next. However, those people soon faded into the background after the threat of additional attacks seemed to diminish. It was certainly true in the city where I live and serve as a pastor. On the Sunday before the attacks, we had 3,834 people attending worship. On the Sunday following the attacks, we had 5,171 people attending worship. For a few weeks this high attendance trend continued. However, on a Sunday six months later, there were 3,816 people attending our worship services. Other pastors reported the same kind of trend that we experienced.

Now I realize that the number of people attending worship can't really measure faith, but the number of people attending church is the only quantitative measure available. It would seem to indicate that millions of Americans felt a desire to call on God after the terrorist attacks, but once the crisis settled down, they no longer felt the need strong enough to attend church. I've been told that the same phenomenon occurred in America on the Sunday after Pearl Harbor with one striking difference. Church attendance remained high throughout WWII. Perhaps that can explained by the fact that the crisis continued.

I hate to even suggest this, but it could be that the next surge in church attendance in America will be on the Sunday after the next terrorist attack on our land. Why? Many people possess a foul-weather faith. Certainly, that kind of faith is better than fair-weather faith, but it's still not the best. Job shows us a more excellent way.

All-Weather Faith: "Whatever happens, I will trust the Lord!"

A person who possesses an all-weather faith says, "Whatever the conditions—sunny, stormy, or partly cloudy—I will trust the Lord." That's the kind of faith that Job had. In Job 1:21, we read what Job said after he learned of the death of his children. *"The Lord gave and the Lord has taken away; may the name of the Lord be praised."* Later in the book, when he was suffering physically and being scorned by his friends, he said, *"Though he slay me, yet will I hope in him"* (Job 13:15).

Remember, Satan's accusation was that if he subjected Job to enough pain, he would curse God to His face. I'm sure there were times when Job was tempted to do that. Satan was constantly whispering in his ear, "Curse God. Surely God doesn't love you if He's letting all this happen to you. Go ahead, curse Him and get it over with." Even Job's wife counseled him to "curse God and die." Later in the book, we'll see that Job asked God some pretty blunt questions and came right to the edge of blasphemy, but he never once cursed God. Genuine, all-weather faith is the only kind of faith that will carry you through to the other side of suffering.

INSIGHT #5: The Object of Your Faith Is More Important Than the Quality of Your Faith!

A great faith in a faulty object is of little use to you. You can stand on the edge of 40-story building and believe with all your heart that an umbrella in your hand will allow you to float down to the street below. However, if you act on that great faith, you will have a rude awakening waiting for you. Yet a little faith in a reliable object is of great worth. Jesus said that if you have just a mustard seed-sized faith, mountains will jump out of your way. The difference in a seed and a mountain is simple: a tiny seed is organic; it has life. A mountain is made of dead rocks: inorganic. A little bit of a living faith in a loving God will sustain you through the darkest seasons of your life.

Tell Me Why?

It was a few days before Christmas in 1978. I was still serving the small congregation of good people where Ray and Jeannette Davis were members. Another couple in our church was waiting for their daughter, son-in-law, and two grandchildren to arrive for a holiday dinner, but the family never arrived. On the way to their house, the car ran off the road and rolled over several times. The young father and children were killed. Only this couple's daughter survived. When I got the phone call, my heart sank as I heard the news. I learned that the family had gathered at the hospital where their daughter had been taken. I'll never forget walking into the ER waiting area. The grandfather was sitting there with his head buried in his hands. I walked over and hugged the grief-stricken grandmother. She looked into my eyes and asked, "Why did God take my babies?" All the other family members looked at me to answer the question.

In the past 30 years, I've since learned that when grieving family members ask a question like that, in that setting, they don't really expect an answer. They're just expressing their grief. However, as a 25-year-old pastor, I mistakenly believed that I should be able to supply all the answers to tough questions. I thought my job was to fill every uncomfortable silence with some appropriate spiritual words. I took a deep breath and made a feeble attempt at some consoling, theological observations. To be honest with you, I don't even remember what I said, but the words seemed hollow in my own ears as I spoke. Of course, my theological observations didn't miraculously transform their anguish into peace. When I finished, nobody said, "Oh, thank you, pastor, we're much better now that we've heard your explanation." Instead, the devastated grandmother continued to weep and cry out, "Why did God take my babies?"

12

Months later, I recall visiting with that same lady. We talked about the dreadful night in the ER, and I asked her if she remembered the words of comfort I shared with her. Naturally, she didn't remember a thing I said. She simply remembered that I was there and that I prayed for them. She had somehow completely forgotten my deep theological observations. In one sense, we're all like Job and this devastated grandmother. In the middle of our suffering and anguish, we want to ask "Why?" We feel that we deserve some reasonable, rational explanation to explain what's happening. However, the truth is that there is no answer. There's just an assurance that God doesn't stop loving us when we suffer.

Finding God's Peace in Your Pain

In the middle of Job's suffering, long before he had his fortune and family restored, he found the peace from God that allowed him to survive. He looked toward heaven and saw the same vision that my arthritic friend Jeannette Davis saw through her veil of tears. They both saw Jesus. Job didn't call Him by name because His name wouldn't be revealed for several centuries. Job simply recognized His role. In Job 19:25 he said, *"I know that my Redeemer lives, and that in the end he will stand upon the earth."* Today we know that our Redeemer's name is Jesus. If you look to Him, He can forgive your sins and give you grace to endure all the trials of life.

One of the reasons Job was able to endure Satan's schemes was because of a supernatural hedge of protection God placed around him. The next chapter shows us why it's available to every believer today, but we must understand how it works and how God provides it.

13

"Because we have lost perspective, we fail to see that unless one is willing to accept suffering properly, he or she is really refusing to continue in the quest for maturity. To refuse suffering is to refuse personal growth."

–Henri J. M. Nouwen

CHAPTER 2

God's Hedge of
Protection

❧

In another of my books, *Do Angels Really Exist?*, I recount the story of missionaries John Pollock and his wife who went to the New Hebrides Islands in the South Pacific. When they arrived, they were the first Europeans that the natives had ever seen. The tribal magician feared these foreign intruders, so he convinced the members of his tribe that these strangers had come to kill the children of their tribe.

One evening, the native warriors surrounded the couple's hut, planning to kill them. Expecting an attack at any moment, the Pollocks stayed on their knees praying for safety all through the night. The night passed and the native warriors never attacked. Over time, the Pollocks learned the local language and won the trust of the people. Many of them came to know Christ. Years later, after the chief of the tribe became a Christian, John said to him, "We have always been curious about the first night we were here. Your tribe surrounded us with your spears, but you didn't attack. Why not?"

The chief replied, "Because of all your guards. Where did you get all those men?"

John said, "It was only my wife and me." The chief responded, "Oh, no. All that evening we saw large men with swords in their hands surrounding your hut. We were afraid so we never attacked."

Like the Pollocks discovered, it's great to know that God can dispatch angels to provide a protective hedge around His servants whenever we experience adversity. And adversity is one of God's most effective teaching tools. The story of Job begins with a description of a man who was happy and wealthy. He owned great riches and enjoyed ten children. Nevertheless, all of that was about to change because of a conversation that took place in heaven between God and Satan. Read this amazing conversation in Job 1:6–12:

> *One day the angels came to present themselves before the Lord, and Satan also came with them. The Lord said to Satan, "Where have you come from?" Satan answered the Lord, "From roaming through the earth and going back and forth in it." Then the Lord said to Satan, "Have you considered my servant Job? There is no one on earth like him; he is blameless and upright, a man who fears God and shuns evil."*

> *"Does Job fear God for nothing?" Satan replied. "Have you not put a hedge around him and his household and everything he has? You have blessed the work of his hands, so that his flocks and herds are spread throughout the land. But stretch out your hand and strike everything he has, and he will surely curse you to your face."*

> *The Lord said to Satan, "Very well, then, everything he has is in your hands, but on the man himself do not lay a finger." Then Satan went out from the presence of the Lord.*

Who Qualifies for a Hedge of Protection?

I've always been fascinated with Satan's claim that God had built a hedge of protection around Job. Maybe you've heard people pray for a "hedge of protection" to be built around someone, but you're not sure what that means. Let's study that concept more closely.

Those Who Honor Him

Did you notice God's evaluation of Job? He said, *"Have you considered my servant Job?"* (Job 1:8), It would be nice to think that God builds a hedge of protection around everyone, but He is looking for people who have surrendered their lives to Him to become His servants. If you want to have a divine hedge protecting you, your first priority should be to become a servant of God.

There are many examples in the Bible of God's promise to protect His servants. For instance, the Bible says, *"His faithfulness will be your shield and your rampart...If you make the Most High your dwelling—even the Lord who is my refuge—then no harm will befall you, no disaster will come near your tent. For he will command his angels concerning you to guard you in all your ways."* (Psalm 91:4, 10–11).

When you hear the word "hedge," what you think of? Most people think of a hedge made of plants. You may have a set of hedge clippers somewhere in your garage that you use to trim hedges in your yard. The word "hedge" in the Bible describes something more substantial than a bush. The Hebrew word means, "wall." A hedge was a military defensive wall built around a city. The base would be comprised of stones or hard, packed dirt with thorny trees on the top. An attacking army would have to climb the hedge and also deal with the thorny barrier before they could breach the wall. In his conversation with God, Satan complained that God had built a similar spiritual hedge around Job. Job couldn't see this hedge, but Satan could. It's a wonderful comfort to realize that God can provide a supernatural barrier around His servants to protect them from spiritual attacks.

God Provides an Individual Hedge

We each need to claim God's promise of personal protection. His protective hedge can only be removed by His express permission. Dr. J. Vernon McGee, the great Bible teacher and long-time radio teacher on "Through the Bible," wrote this about God's hedge: "I believe there is a hedge around every believer today, and I do not think that Satan can touch you unless God permits it. And if God permits it, it will be for His purpose."[1]

Are you praying for a hedge of protection around those you love? If you're a parent or a grandparent, you should be praying for an individual hedge of protection around your children and grandchildren. Husbands and wives, you can pray for God to put a hedge around your mate so that they will stay faithful to you. The story of Hosea and Gomer in the Old Testament illustrates this key truth. Hosea's wife, Gomer, was an adulteress. When she wandered away from her husband, God put up a hedge to keep her from being unfaithful. The entire story is an allegory of how Israel had tried to be unfaithful to God. God said, *"Therefore I will hedge her way with thornbushes; I will wall her in so that she cannot find her way. She will chase after her lovers but not catch them...then she will say, 'I will go back to my husband as at first, for I was better off than now'"* (Hosea 2:6–7). If your mate is working or traveling in an area where there is sexual temptation, you should pray for God to hedge him or her in! Your spouse may get "stuck" by God's thornbush, but that's much better than being stuck in sin!

Job was the kind of father who prayed for a hedge of protection around each of his children. Job 1:5 says, *"Early in the morning he would sacrifice a burnt offering for each of them, thinking, 'Perhaps my children have sinned and cursed God in their hearts.' This was Job's regular custom"* (Job 1:5). Job realized that God had called him to be the spiritual leader of his family.

Men, are you being a good spiritual leader for your family? Is it your regular custom to worship and pray and intercede on behalf of your family? Guys, if you want to be a spiritual leader, the first thing you must do is to start praying for your family, beginning with asking God for a hedge of protection around them.

God Provides a National Hedge

I believe that God can place a hedge of protection around a nation as well. Since our nation's birth, it's obvious that God's hand of blessing has been on us. Because people who feared

God and acknowledged Him as the source of all liberty and freedom founded our nation, God placed a hedge of protection around our country.

That hedge was violated on September 11, 2001. The terrorist attacks weren't just a wake-up call for us; they were a kneel-down call to America. The Bible says, *"Blessed is the nation who God is the Lord"* (Psalm 33:12). Scripture is clear about what happens to nations who reject God. *"The wicked shall be turned into hell, and all the nations that forget God"* (Psalm 9:17).

Historical revisionists are trying to rewrite American history to remove any reference to God or the Bible. They are doing it to promote their secular humanist philosophy and to justify their own godless lifestyle. These revisionists know that if they can successfully remove God and the Bible from the public forum, they can omit the troubling truth concerning moral outrages like legalized abortion. We read in the Bible where God says that He knew us in the womb and that He hates hands that shed innocent blood.

While all of our founding fathers weren't evangelicals, they honored and revered God. Consider the words that George Washington spoke at his presidential inauguration on April 30, 1789: "It would be peculiarly improper to omit, in this first official act, my fervent supplication to that Almighty Being, who rules over the universe, who presides in the councils of nations, and whose providential aid can supply every human defect, that His benediction may consecrate to the liberties and happiness of the people of the United States...We ought to be no less persuaded that the propitious smiles of Heaven can never be expected on a nation that disregards the eternal rules of order and right, which Heaven itself has ordained."[2]

We live in a time when we talk a lot about homeland security. We need something much more important than that; we need heavenly security. The Church of the Lord Jesus Christ should be the Department of Heavenly Security! Let's pray that our nation will remain one nation under God—and one nation under God's protection.

Who's to Blame?

Satan asked, *"Does Job fear God for nothing?...Have you not put a hedge around him and his household and everything he has?...stretch out your hand and strike everything he has, and he will surely curse you to your face"* (Job 1:9–11). Satan implied that the only reason Job honored God was because God had bribed him. He was insinuating that God cannot be loved unless He buys that love. God knew Job's heart. He knew that Job would still love Him even if he lost it all. Satan suggested that God test this theory and strike Job, but God never did because God is a good God. He just allowed Satan to carry out a test.

I've known people who express anger at God when they go through times of pain and suffering. I know the feeling, but it is misplaced anger. If you want to express your anger and hatred, direct it at Satan—he is the source of all sickness and suffering. In his book, *Don't Waste Your Sorrows*, Paul Billheimer wrote: "Satan is the agent of destruction, not God. Who was it that destroyed Job's fortune, family, and health when God permitted it done? Satan. Satan brings about accidents, sickness, disease, and calamity, and then tempts men to think that God brings these things to pass. Thus millions blame God for the work of the devil, even some Christians who should know better. The permission of God is never the same as the evil work of Satan after permission is granted him; withdrawing protection is not the same as the destruction itself. God's work is that of deliverance; Satan's is that of destruction."[3]

Weapons of Satan's Destruction

Job faced Satan's attack and survived. Of course, Job didn't have access to all the biblical truth we have today. The Bible says that we are to *"resist the devil and he will flee"* from us (James 4:17). How do we resist the devil? We have an advantage over Job because we have plenty of scriptures that teach us how to withstand Satan's attacks. We see the saints that make it through the horrific time of tribulation in the end times overcome Satan this way: *"Now have come the salvation and the power and the kingdom of our God, and the authority of his Christ. For the accuser of our brothers, who accuses them before our God day and night, has been hurled down. They overcame him by the blood of the Lamb and by the word of their testimony; they did not love their lives so much as to shrink from death"* (Revelation 12:10). This verse in Revelation gives us three powerful weapons to use against Satan. You're familiar with WMDs, weapons of mass destruction, because of the news media. I call these three secret weapons WSDs: Weapons of Satan's Destruction. When Satan attacks, you can:

(1) Refer him to Calvary
We are first told in Revelation 12 that the tribulation saints overcame Satan *"by the blood of the Lamb."* By His death on the cross, Jesus built a hedge of eternal protection around us. In Exodus 12, God told the Israelites to sacrifice a male lamb without spot or blemish and smear its blood on the door posts and lentils of their homes. Afterward, the family would go into their house, roast the lamb, and eat it. God promised that when the Destroyer (an angel) came, he would pass over every house where God saw the blood of the lamb. That's why this event is called "Passover" today.

That is an illustration of what Jesus did for you at Calvary. He was the spotless Lamb of God who went to the cross to redeem us from our sin. When His blood is applied to our hearts, it forms a hedge of protection against God's judgement against sin.

(2) Remember your confession
Revelation 12 also explains that the saints who make it through the tribulation overcome Satan through *"the word of their testimony."* I think this refers to two things. First, there is the written Word of testimony, the Bible. There is great power in quoting the Word of God. When the devil tempted Jesus in the wilderness, He defeated him by quoting three little known verses from Deuteronomy. What do you think we could do

21

quoting passages from the Gospels or Romans?

However, this confession also refers to your *experienced* "word of testimony." In other words, whenever we give witness to our faith, the devil is shamed and defeated. You should give your testimony to others, to Satan, to yourself, and even to God! Every time you quote Scripture and share your testimony it's like sucker-punching the old devil in the stomach.

(3) Renew your commitment

The third weapon of Satan's destruction is total commitment to Jesus. It says of those over-comers in Revelation 12 that *"they did not love their lives so much as to shrink from death."* Another weapon against which Satan has no defense is a surrendered life. Some people think of Job as a man who lost it all, but I think of him differently. I see a man who came to see that the one thing he had left was the only thing he needed: his relationship with his Redeemer. Yes, Job lost his fortune, his family, his fitness, his friends, and he even lost face, but the one thing he did not lose was his faith. He was willing to trust God even if he died. In Job 13:15 he said, *"Though he slay me, yet will I praise Him."*

The secret to victory over the devil is to live life abandoned to God. Most of our worries stem from the fact that we love our lives so much that we are afraid of dying. Satan uses this fear of death to intimidate us throughout our lives. However, you can't scare a dead man. Jesus said, *"If any man will come after me, let him deny himself, and take up his cross daily and follow me"* (Luke 9:23). Sometimes when people suffer they say, "I guess it's just a cross I have to bear." Bearing the cross doesn't mean living with acid reflux or an ingrown toenail. Bearing a cross means death. In Bible times, when you saw a man carrying a cross you knew one thing for certain: he was going to his death. Like a prisoner walking from death row to the chamber to receive a lethal injection, Job was a dead man walking. When you're fully committed to Jesus Christ, you can have that same kind of fearlessness.

Are You within God's Hedge?

Satan is always trying to breach God's hedge of protection. However, unless God had allowed Satan to test Job, he never could have touched him. When our faith is firm and we pass the test, God establishes the hedge even stronger than it was before.

If you know the Lord, I believe you'll see Job in heaven. Not because he was a good man, but because he was a man who put his trust in God. People in the Old Testament weren't saved by keeping the law. If that was the case, then none of them would qualify for heaven. People in the Old Testament experienced salvation the very same way that you can be saved today: by placing their faith and trust in Jesus.

How can that be if the New Testament wasn't yet written? Job put his faith in Jesus, even though he didn't know His name. Picture where Job was when he placed his faith in Christ. Sitting on an ash heap. Scraping his sores with a broken piece of pottery. His wife and friends were making his life even more miserable. Still, at the darkest moment, he found peace in the middle of pain. By faith, he saw that his loving heavenly Father would provide a Redeemer for him. Remember Job 19:25 when he said, *"I know that my Redeemer lives, and that in the end he will stand upon the earth."* Notice Job didn't say "a redeemer"; he said, "My redeemer." It's one thing to say that Jesus is Lord; it's another to confess that Jesus is *my* Lord. It's one thing to say that Jesus is the Savior of the world; it's another to say that Jesus is *my* Savior. King David didn't say, "The Lord is a shepherd." He said, "The Lord is *my* shepherd."

Can you say that today? Have you turned from your sins and placed your faith in Jesus? Then and only then can you expect to experience the benefits and blessings of God's hedge of protection even when your world is crumbling all around you. When you experience that kind of heavy-duty fallout in life, you will be desperate for help. The next part of Job's story tells us step by step what to do when our world falls apart.

"...There is suffering in life, and there are defeats. No one can avoid them. But it's better to lose some of the battles in the struggles for your dreams than to be defeated without ever knowing what you're fighting for."

–Paulo Coelho

CHAPTER 3

What to Do When Your World Crumbles

One day a man in Florida was working on his motorcycle, which was parked outside on his patio. He was racing the engine to diagnose what was wrong when his hand slipped off the clutch. The motorcycle lurched forward through their glass door, with the man still hanging onto the handlebars for dear life. Upon hearing the commotion, his wife rushed in and found her husband, conscious but bleeding from several scrapes. She dialed 911 and paramedics soon arrived to transport her wounded husband to the ER. Meanwhile, the wife saw that gasoline was leaking out of the motorcycle onto the carpet. She blotted it up with a handful of paper towels, disposing them in the toilet.

Later that day, the man returned home all bandaged up. Feeling despondent about the broken glass and his motorcycle lying like a wounded animal in his living room, he sought solace in the bathroom. He lit a cigarette and when he finished, tossed it into the toilet. You got it—the same toilet that had been filled earlier with the gasoline-soaked paper towels! The force from the explosion shattered the toilet and threw the unfortunate smoker out the bathroom door. His wife found him lying face-down with burns on the back of his legs. For the second time that day, she dialed 911 and met the same paramedic crew at the door to transport her husband. As they were carrying him down the steps to the ambulance, one of the EMTs asked the wife what had happened. When she told them the story, they began to laugh so hard that one of them slipped and dropped the stretcher, dumping her husband on the steps where he broke his arm. I'm not completely sure all the facts of that story are accurate, but that's what I call having a bad day!

Bad days come in all shapes and sizes. From the cradle to the grave, we experience painful situations that bring tears to our eyes. As followers of Jesus Christ, every tear is a reminder that there will be a place and time when pain will cease and God will wipe away every tear from our eyes. The more pain we experience in this life, the more we long for that other world. Oxford scholar C.S. Lewis wrote, "If I find in myself a desire which no experience in this world can satisfy, the most probable explanation is that I was made for another world."[4]

The Day Job's World Crumbled in

Keep the end of the story in the back of your mind and you consider the details of Job's loss. Job endured all the pain and trials that the devil tossed his way and never lost his faith. In the end, God restored to him *more* than he ever had in the first place. With that caveat, let's read about the day Job's world crumbled in Job 1:13–22:

> *One day when Job's sons and daughters were feasting and drinking wine at the oldest brother's house, a messenger came to Job and said, "The oxen were plowing and the donkeys were grazing nearby, and the Sabeans attacked and carried them off. They put the servants to the sword, and I am the only one who has escaped to tell you!" While he was yet speaking, another messenger came and said, "The fire of God fell from the sky and burned up the sheep and the servants, and I am the only one who has escaped to tell you!" While he was yet speaking, another messenger came and said, "The Chaldeans formed three raiding parties and swept down on your camels and*

carried them off. They put the servants to the sword, and I am the only one who has escaped to tell you!" While he was still speaking, yet another messenger came and said, "Your sons and daughters were feasting and drinking wine at the oldest brother's house, when suddenly a mighty wind swept in from the desert and struck the four corners of the house. It collapsed on them and they are dead, and I am the only one who has escaped to tell you!" At this, Job got up and tore his robe and shaved his head. Then he fell to the ground in worship and said, "Naked I came from my mother's womb, and naked I will depart. The Lord gave and the Lord has taken away; may the name of the Lord be praised." In all this, Job did not sin by charging God with wrongdoing.

Grief-recovery experts have developed a simple equation to explain grief: Change + Loss = Grief. Job's life changed drastically on the single day that he experienced both material and personal loss. Like many Texas ranchers, Job invested his wealth in his livestock. I added up the total number of different kinds of livestock Job lost and compared it to the current price in today's market. I discovered that Job's livestock was worth approximately $40 million. (Remember, he had 7,000 camels? A single camel sells for $15,000 in Saudi Arabia today.) Can you imagine the pain of losing your entire net worth in one day?

Yet his personal loss was much more devastating than his financial loss. His three daughters and seven sons were all in the same house when a severe storm blew in. The walls of the building collapsed, killing them instantly. On the heels of hearing about his financial blow out, Job learned that his children were also dead. As we walk through seasons of grief and pain in our lives, we would be wise to notice how Job responded when his world crumbled.

Express Your Grief Honestly

The first thing Job teaches us about grief is to express it honestly and openly. Job expressed his agonizing grief in three ways. First, he ripped his clothing. Tearing ones clothes was a customary way of expressing immediate grief in the ancient world. Tearing cloth is a metaphor for a broken heart. There's the strain of pulling and the release when the cloth tears. Most of us can relate to a time when we felt so much emotional pain that we wished we could tear something or slam our fist through a wall.

Job also shaved his head. Tearing his clothes was an immediate expression of his grief, but the shaving of his head was a long term expression of his pain. Every time he felt his bare head and the chill on his scalp, he remembered his grief. As his hair grew out, it was also a gradual reminder to him that life goes on and that with time, the pain lessens. Cancer survivors have told me that when their hair started growing out after chemotherapy, the gradual change in their appearance was a daily reminder that life was returning to a new normal. I'm not recommending that we start shaving our heads when we experience grief. However, it would help if we had some tangible way to see that the pain of our grief was slowly receding.

Third, Job collapsed to the ground when he got the bad news. You might have had a similar experience of hearing such bad news that you lost the strength to stand. However, Job didn't collapse into helplessness or hopelessness; he fell down to worship God. Whenever you hurt, it's important to express your grief honestly. Grief that is submerged or suppressed can lead to unhealthy emotional problems. Job didn't deny his grief. He didn't slap a fake smile on his face and flippantly say, "Everything is going to be okay." We don't specifically read in this first chapter that Job wept, but you have to imagine the dirt beneath him was wet with tears as he worshiped God. In chapter 16, Job admitted how deeply he was grieving. He said, *"I have sewed sackcloth over my skin and buried my brow in the dust. My face is red with weeping, deep shadows ring my eyes"* (vv15–16).

28

The Greater the Loss, the Greater the Pain

When you lose anything you value, you grieve. The greater the sense of loss, the greater the depth of your grief. Parents have told me that there is nothing to compare with the depth of grief over the death of a child. However, death isn't the only thing that causes grief. When you lose a job, you grieve. When you lose a mate through divorce or death, you grieve. When you lose a friend, or lose a house, or lose your freedom, you grieve. Whatever the nature of your loss, it's important to express your grief honestly.

It doesn't show a lack of faith to cry a river of tears. The Bible says that Christians experience sorrow, but we don't sorrow as those who have no hope. That is a key difference. Even in the midst of our pain and loss, we still have hope. Jesus was called a Man of Sorrows and well-acquainted with grief. He wept out of compassion for Mary and Martha at their brother's grave, despite the fact that within minutes He planned to resuscitate Lazarus. Jesus was so heartbroken over the sinful people in Jerusalem that He stood on a hill overlooking the city and wept bitter tears for them. It's not merely okay to grieve; in fact, it's good to grieve.

Acknowledge Every Blessing as a Gift from God

The second lesson we learn from Job's pain is that he acknowledged that everything he had was a gift from God. Three key words stand out in v21: *"The Lord gave ... "* He admitted that he entered the world naked, and he would leave it the same way he came. These days, we still come into the world naked, but many people are buried in a $500 suit. Regardless of your stock portfolio on earth, you'll enter the afterlife with zero material assets. I've done hundreds of funerals over the years, and I've never seen a U-Haul following the hearse in a funeral procession.

I've known people who made the mistake of thinking that everything good in their lives came to them because they *earned* it. They think that society owes them a living, or that they deserve to have all their needs met. Sadly, many people rarely glance up and acknowledge the source of their blessings. However, the Bible teaches clearly that everything good in life is a gift that comes from God above. *"Every good and perfect gift is from above, coming down from the Father of the heavenly lights, who does not change like shifting shadows"* (James 1:17). The story of Job took place almost 4,000 years ago, but the same God who had a personal relationship with Job wants to have a personal relationship with you. The Bible says, *"The wages of sin is death, but the **gift** of God is eternal life through Jesus Christ our Lord"* (Romans 6:23). That's the greatest gift you can receive—and no one can ever take it from you.

God May Take Something Away without Giving You a Reason
Third, we must accept the fact that God has the right to take anything at anytime; after all, it's His world. Before the end of the story, Job will ask God "Why?" in a variety of ways. Although God responds to Job, He doesn't give him any answers. As far as we know, God never even let Job in on the deal that took place with the devil. Instead, God simply reminds Job that His wisdom, greatness, and power are far beyond anyone's ability to comprehend.

In the book of Romans, Paul is writing about God's plan for the ages when he breaks out in this observation, *"Oh, the depth of the riches of the wisdom and knowledge of God! How unsearchable are his judgments, and his paths beyond tracing out! Who has known the mind of the Lord? Or been his counselor? Who has ever given to God that God should repay him?"* (Romans 11:33–35). If you've experienced tragedy and you think you deserve an answer to the question, "Why did this happen?" your concept of God is too small. There will always be a sense of mystery and awe about Him.

When you've lost something or someone precious it's easy to forget what Job said: the Lord gives and the Lord takes away. John Claypool was a respected pastor where I went to seminary in Louisville, Kentucky. He and his wife lost a little daughter, Laura Lou, to leukemia at a young age. He often explained his loss by telling a story from his childhood. During WWII, his family didn't own a washing machine. Gas was rationed and they couldn't afford to drive to a laundromat. Keeping their clothes clean became a challenge. When their neighbor went into the service and his wife moved in with her family, they offered to let John's family use their Bendix wringer washer while they were gone rather than to let it sit rusting on the porch.

John helped with the family laundry and developed a fondness for the old green machine that his family had moved into their house. However, when the war ended, his neighbors returned. Over the course of the war, young John had actually forgotten that the machine was on loan to them. When the neighbors removed it, John was upset and even angry that they would take "his" washing machine. His mother sat him down and said, "John, you must remember that the washing machine never belonged to us in the first place. That we ever got to use it at all was a gift. So, instead of being mad at it being taken away, let's be thankful that we ever had it at all."

As a father, John would say that he struggled with the death of his child until he remembered that old green Bendix. He wrote, "When I remember that Laura Lou was a gift, pure and simple, something I neither earned nor deserved nor had a right to; and when I remember that the appropriate response to a gift, even when it is taken away, is gratitude, then I am better able to try and thank God that I was ever given her in the first place."[5] That's exactly how Job felt. He knew that every good thing in his life had come from God, and that God had the right to take anything away. That's the kind of balanced attitude that will keep you from becoming bitter when you face loss.

When You Don't Feel Like It, Faith It

Have you ever heard the advice, "Cheer up, things could be worse?" Job cheered up, and sure enough things got worse! In the next chapter, we're going to see how Job's pain and suffering actually intensifies as Satan attacks his health. Instead of assessing blame, Job chooses to express praise to God. He says in v21, *"May the name of the Lord be praised."* However, what do you think Job *felt* like doing?

We know what Mrs. Job felt like doing. In Job 2:9 she told

Job to *"curse God and die."* Job probably shared her feelings, but he didn't live by his feelings. He lived by his faith. Even when you're hurting, you can still make the choice to praise God. How? Don't fake it; faith it. Praise God by faith for how He is going to comfort you and provide for you in the midst of your pain.

It's easy to offer praise to God when everything is wonderful in your life. However, when you offer God praise in the midst of your pain, it becomes a precious sacrifice. The Bible says, *"Through Jesus, therefore, let us continually offer to God a sacrifice of praise—the fruit of lips that confess his name"* (Hebrews 13:15).

Caution! Contents under Pressure

God taught me a lesson a few days ago from the strangest source. I was getting ready to shave and noticed the label on the side of the can of shaving cream. It said, "Caution! Contents under pressure. Do not incinerate or puncture." If you burn or puncture a can of shaving cream, the high pressure will cause the can to explode.

That label describes what a lot of people are going through these days. They are living under intense pressure and stress, and they may be only a few degrees away from an explosion. They can't stand the heat and they don't know how to get out of the kitchen. If you want to know what's really inside a person's heart, see what comes out when they are under pressure.

The fundamental issue of the book of Job is this question: "If I lose everything that I hold dear, what's left to sustain me?" If your sense of worth and happiness is defined by your possessions, then prepare to be devastated. However, if your sense of worth and joy is based upon a living relationship with a loving God, nothing in this universe can separate you from His love.

When you're hurting and about to explode emotionally, try following Job's example. Express your grief honestly; don't suppress it. Acknowledge that every good gift in your life has come from God. In the midst of your pain, even when you don't feel like it, offer praise to God. One thing we should *not do* when our world crumbles in is blame God. Notice the last words in chapter 1: *"In all this, Job did not sin by charging God with*

32

wrongdoing." Whenever we suffer, we immediately look for someone to blame. If we can blame our suffering on our parents, our spouse, our co-workers, or society in general, then we can justify our bitterness. That bitterness prevents us from moving on and becoming whole again. God gets unjustly blamed for a lot of suffering today. However, in spite of his pain, and his unanswered questions, Job never charged that God was wrong. Surely Job was afraid of what was still to come, but from the very beginning of his pain he put his trust firmly in God.

Before Columbus sailed to the New World, the common belief was that if a ship from Europe sailed too far west, it would either fall off the edge of the world or face terrible danger. In England, there is an ancient nautical map that dates back to the time of King Henry IV. On it, the map makers noted their fear of the unknown, writing these words over the Atlantic Ocean: "Here be dragons; here be demons; here be danger."

Based on those superstitious warnings, most sailors were afraid of sailing there. Nevertheless, an English navigator by the name of John Franklin (who was a mighty man of God) knew that God sits above the circle of the earth. He took that same map and crossed out those fearful words with three words of his own: "Here be God!" If you are a servant of God sailing toward your darkest fears and deepest worries, remember: "Here be God!" He is already there to keep you, sustain you, and give you peace in the middle of your pain.

Our universe is so large that scientists can't measure it. However, the Bible says in Isaiah 40:12 that God measures the heavens with the span of His hand. Therefore, when your world crumbles in, the most important thing you can do is to place yourself in God's hands. As you may have learned when you were little, the safest place in this world is in His hands. However, just because you know that's true, it doesn't mean you won't still have doubts. And sometimes in the middle of the night, when the pain seems the most intense, you may even wonder, "Would I be better off dead?" Job wondered the same thing. I have a definitive answer that to that question in the next chapter.

33

"Pain is temporary. It may last a minute, or an hour, or a day, or a year, but eventually it will subside and something else will take its place. If I quit, however, it lasts forever."

–Lance Armstrong

CHAPTER 4

Would I Be
Better off Dead?

I heard about a wealthy Texas oil man who was getting married. He was the nervous type, so before the wedding he told the preacher, "Preacher, the shorter you make this ceremony, the more I'm going to pay you." The preacher thought for a moment as he waited for the bride to enter. Then as the couple stood at the altar, he asked the groom, "Take her?" Then to the startled bride he asked, "Take him?" They both nodded and the preacher pronounced them, "Took!" The world's shortest marriage ceremony—only in Texas!

In some ways, this could be the world's shortest chapter. When it comes to the question, "Would I be better off dead?" I have a short answer. Yes and no—it all depends. If you're a Christian, then yes, heaven is preferable to life. Only you don't get to set your departure time. If you're not a Christian, then no, you wouldn't be better off dead. You still have time to respond to Christ's offer of eternal life. Rather than stopping at a simplistic answer, let's consider the question in more detail because it has flashed through many people's minds when they're suffering. Including Job's.

After round one of Satan's withering attack against Job, the score stood like this: Job 1; Satan 0. However, the devil wasn't finished yet. After the loss of Job's wealth and family, his next weapon was physical suffering. We read about it in Job 2:1–10:

On another day, the angels came to present themselves before the Lord, and Satan also came with them to present himself before him. And the Lord said to Satan, "Where have you come from?" Satan answered the Lord, "From roaming through the earth and going back and forth in it." Then the Lord said to Satan, "Have you considered my servant Job? There is no one on earth like him; he is blameless and upright, a man who fears God and shuns evil. And he still maintains his integrity, though you incited me against him to ruin him without any reason." "Skin for skin!" Satan replied. "A man will give all he has for his own life. But stretch out your hand and strike his flesh and bones, and he will surely curse you to your face." The Lord said to Satan, "Very well, then, he is in your hands; but you must spare his life." So Satan went out from the presence of the Lord and afflicted Job with painful sores from the soles of his feet to the top of his head. Then Job took a piece of broken pottery and scraped himself with it as he sat among the ashes. His wife came to him, "Are you still holding on to your integrity? Curse God and die!" He replied, "You are talking like a foolish woman. Shall we accept good from God and not trouble?" In all this, Job did not sin in what he said.

Although Job didn't sin, he felt like dying. The desperate cry of a tormented soul says in 3:11–13, *"Why did I not perish at birth and die as I came from the womb? Why were there knees to receive me and breasts that I might be nursed? For now I would be lying down in peace; I would be asleep and at rest..."* Have you ever felt like saying, "I wish I had never

36

been born in the first place"? In vv20–26, Job suggests that death would be preferable to this misery. *"Why is light given to those in misery, and life to bitter of soul, to those who long for death that does not come, who search for it more than for hidden treasure, who are filled with gladness and rejoice when they reach the grave? Why is life given to a man whose way is hidden, whom God has hedged in? For sighing comes to me instead of food; my groans pour out like water. What I feared has come upon me; what I dreaded has happened to me. I have no peace, no quietness; I have no rest, but only turmoil."*

Maybe you've never expressed it exactly in those words, but at some time, most of us have wondered if we wouldn't be better off dead. As we deal with these painful feelings, there are some helpful lessons we can gather from Job's story.

LESSON 1: Satan Is Persistent in His Attack

You've got to give the devil his due: he is persistent. Even though Job survived round one, the devil wasn't satisfied until he gained God's permission for round two and attacked Job's health. For all his persistence, the devil isn't all that creative; he is still attacking God's servants today using the same methods he used on Job.

Satan May Attack Your Health

Satan afflicted Job with sores so painful that all he could do to deal with the pain was to scrape the sores with a pottery shard. Later, Job would describe his physical suffering: *"My body is clothed with worms and scabs, my skin is broken and festering"* (Job 7:5). That's not to say that every sickness is a direct attack from Satan; we live in a fallen world with sickness and sin. However, when permitted, Satan may try to attack our health. In 2 Corinthians 12, the Apostle Paul complained about a painful thorn in his flesh. It was some kind of physical suffering or he wouldn't have described it as a part of his flesh. We don't know what it was, but Paul said it was *"a messenger of Satan to torment me"* (2 Corinthians 12:7). When the Apostle Peter was telling Cornelius about Jesus, he said that Jesus went about *"healing those who were afflicted by the devil"* (Acts 10:38). Satan wants to make you miserable, and sometimes he does it by attacking your health.

Satan May Attack Your Marriage

Some male Bible scholars have added with a chuckle that Job lost his fortune, his family, and his fitness, and to add to his suffering, his wife survived! Satan is a crafty old dog. In order to get to you, he isn't above attacking or using those closest to you (as he did with Job's children and wife). Remember Satan alleged before God that Job would curse Him—exactly what Mrs. Job suggested (Job 2:9).

Before we get too critical of her, we must remember that Mrs. Job had also suffered greatly. She was under a tremendous amount of stress herself. She had just lost ten children and watched as her mate suffered financial ruin and physical pain. Satan uses adversity to drive a wedge between husbands and wives instead of bringing them closer together to comfort each other. Job admonished his wife, "You are talking like a foolish woman." He didn't call his wife a fool; he said she was talking like a foolish woman. In the Bible, a fool is someone who *"says in their heart, 'there is no God'"* (Psalm 53:1). Job's wife believed in God, but she spoke foolishly about Him, as if God should be blamed for their suffering. Fortunately, Job's wife stayed with him, and in the end she also enjoyed the blessings of God. So, don't let Satan succeed by hurting you through those who love you.

LESSON 2: Even God's Faithful Servants May Sometimes Feel Like Quitting

I like Eugene Petersen's paraphrase of Job's words: *"Why does God bother keeping the bitter people alive? Those who want in the worst way to die, and can't? Who can't imagine anything better than death? Who count the day of their death and burial the happiest day of their life?"* (Job 3:20–21, The Message)

Some of the questions and statements from Job and his friends wander to the very edge of blasphemy. Job was just expressing the depth of his pain. He was bemoaning the truth that sometimes the sufferings of this life can become so painful that we long for the next life. Elijah expressed similar agony the day he sat under a tree and complained to God, *"I have had enough, Lord. Take my life"* (1 Kings 19:4). Also, Jeremiah felt the same way when he said, *"Cursed be the day I was born! Why did I ever come out of the womb to see trouble and sorrow?"* (Jeremiah 20:14, 18). Even God's most faithful servants have expressed the same kind of agonizing frustration that Job (and perhaps you) experienced.

I've been serving as a pastor for over three decades, and people often ask me, "Pastor, have you ever felt that way?" My answer is usually, "Not more than four or five times a day!" Of course I've gone through periods of time when I longed to go, more than to stay. It's okay to look at life's pain compared with the joys of heaven and say, "I'd be better off dead." That may be true, but that doesn't mean that we have the right to seriously contemplate ending our lives or quitting on God. Elijah didn't quit; Jeremiah didn't quit; Job didn't quit; I'm not quitting, and don't you give up, either!

Let's Go to the Movies

I believe there are some rich spiritual truths in many of the movies we watch—we're just often too dull (or full of popcorn) to notice them! Unless you've been hiding in a cave somewhere, chances are you've seen the movie, "It's a Wonderful Life" starring Jimmy Stewart and Donna Reed. When Frank Capra released the movie in 1946, it was a box office flop. Since then, however, it has become a Christmastime favorite.

The movie centers on the character of George Bailey. Life has become so painful for George that he runs away from his family on a snowy Christmas Eve. He sits in a bar over a drink and prays, "Dear Father, I'm not a praying man, but if you're up there and you can hear me, show me the way. I'm at the end

39

of my rope. Show me the way, oh God." After his prayer, the guy next to him, who is the husband of his daughter's teacher, punches George out for insulting his wife on the phone earlier that evening. Outside George rubs his bloodied lip and says, "That's what I get for praying." What a commentary on prayer and suffering! Have you ever felt that way? You're at the bottom of the barrel. You pray for things to get better, and just when you think things can't get any worse, the bottom of the barrel falls out!

Clutching his life insurance policy, George decides that it would better for everyone if he was dead. We see him standing on the edge of a bridge, gazing down into the icy waters. As the snowflakes swirl down toward the rushing river below, George is on the verge of giving up and committing suicide.

At precisely that moment, God's answer to his prayer arrives. Clarence, a goofy guardian angel dispatched from heaven, falls into the river and George has to rescue him. Clarence didn't look much like an angel, nor did he seem like the answer to George's prayer. I've since learned that much of the time when God answers our prayers, we don't always recognize it!

In his conversation with Clarence, George moans, "This world would be a better place if I'd never been born!" In response, Clarence devises a heavenly plan to reveal to George exactly what life would have been like if, indeed, he'd never been born. In one memorable scene, George visits a cemetery and sees the tombstone of his brother: "Harry Bailey 1911-1919." Earlier in the movie, George had rescued Harry from an icy sledding accident. George looks at the tombstone and objects, "That can't be true! Harry's a hero—he flew in the war. He saved all those people on the transport." Clarence sadly reports, "Every man on that transport died. Harry wasn't there to save them because you weren't there to save Harry."

Then Clarence gives the most powerful line in the entire movie: "Strange isn't it? Each man's life touches so many other lives. When he isn't around, he leaves an awful hole, doesn't he?"

Not long after that, we see George on his knees saying, "Help me, Clarence. Get me back. I don't care what happens to me. I want to live again. I want to live again! Dear God, let me live again." I would tell you how the movie ends, but you already know, and besides, I'm starting to shed tears on my laptop! You may be thinking, "My life isn't very wonderful. Nobody cares about me. Nobody would even miss me if I died." Like George, we have no idea how many lives our lives have touched. In your pain, you might forget the people who care for you, and more than that, you might forget your heavenly Father cares.

LESSON 3: You Can Maintain Your Spiritual Integrity during Suffering

Mrs. Job asked her husband, *"Are you still holding on to your integrity? Curse God and die!"* Job not only refused to curse God, he also maintained his integrity throughout his ordeal. Even though the devil is persistent in his attack against you, it's possible for you to maintain your integrity all the while.

The English word "integrity" has almost lost its meaning in today's dog-eat-dog world. Integrity is defined as the quality or condition of being whole or undivided. (It's from the Latin word *integritas,* from *integer*). Let's start with the word "integer" to understand the meaning of integrity. In math, an integer is a whole number. That means that it can't be a fraction or a number that can be divided. For example, 17 is an integer because it can't be evenly divided, but 18 can be divided and, therefore, isn't an integer. To maintain your integrity means that your mind and heart are not divided; they are whole. In the context of Job, integrity means that you fully trust God without a divided heart or a fractured mind. How can you find the ability to have integrity in the middle of your pain? Keep reading.

Trust God's Plan When You Can't See His Hand

At the very moment Job assumed that God had forgotten about him, God was actually devoting personal, almost microscopic attention to Job. Job had no clue that he was the subject of

God's conversation with Satan. In one sense, the God of the Universe was staking His entire divine reputation on how Job would respond to suffering. In contrast, Satan had declared before thousands and perhaps millions of heavenly creatures that Job would break down and curse God when he suffered enough. God, who knows all things, was confident that Job would trust Him.

Like Job, we sometimes can't understand the details surrounding our situation. Even though we don't always *know* God's plan, we just have to *trust* that God has a plan. Job didn't even know God had a plan until the end of the story when he observed, *"I know that you can do all things; no plan of yours can be thwarted"* (Job 42:2). In most cases, you simply have to believe God even when there seems to be no visible evidence of His presence or power in your life. Though often invisible, God is always there.

I think one of the best television shows ever produced was the Andy Griffith show. In one particular episode, we learn the meaning of trust when Andy's son, Opie, tells his father about a friend he met in the forest named Mr. McBeavy. He describes Mr. McBeavy in ways that make him sound like an imaginary alien. Opie claims that Mr. McBeavy came down out of a tree wearing a big shiny hat. He jingled when he walked and he could make smoke come out of his ears. Andy and Opie go search in the woods, but they find no evidence of Mr. McBeavy. Opie stubbornly insists that his friend is real, but Andy is convinced that Opie is just telling stories.

One day, Opie brings in a hatchet that he says Mr. McBeavy gave him. Andy assumes Opie stole it and demands that he return it to the rightful owner. Another day, Opie brings home a quarter that he claims Mr. McBeavy game him. By this point, Andy is angry at Opie—convinced that he is lying and stealing. Finally, Andy gets so frustrated that he sits Opie down and requires him to admit that he made up the whole story about Mr. McBeavy or he will be punished. Opie refuses. He looks at his dad and says, "But he's real, Paw, don't you believe me?"

Andy thinks for a minute, looks his son in the eyes, and says, "Yes, son I believe you." When Barney learns that Andy didn't punish Opie, he's indignant. He says, "Oh come on, Andy, you don't believe in Mr. McBeavy, do you?" In the best line of the show, Andy says, "No, Barn, I don't believe in Mr. McBeavy, but I do believe in Opie."

Later Andy discovers that Mr. McBeavy is actually a forester, working high in the trees with a jingly belt full of tools and wearing a silver hat. Andy was willing to believe in Mr. McBeavy because he believed that his son wouldn't lie to him. When I saw that episode, I immediately applied it to trusting a God that we can't see. Even when we try to tell our friends and family that He's real, they sometimes scoff at our "imaginary friend." Nevertheless, we know He is real. If you're in the midst of suffering and you can't see any evidence of God's *hand*, that's when you just have to trust His *plan*.

Trust God's Grace When You Can't See His Face

When we are hurting, our first response is to beg God to change our circumstances. However, if you only focus on your painful circumstances, you are zeroing in on the wrong thing. Instead, shift your spiritual gaze to God. Start looking around to see what God is doing. Even though you might not see His face, you can trust His grace.

I've often heard people attribute a popular phrase to the Bible: "God moves in mysterious ways." Actually, that phrase isn't in the Bible at all. The words ring true, but they come from the lyrics of a great hymn written by William Cowper. My favorite verse is the third one, but if grew up in a Baptist church you usually only sang the first, second, and last stanza! The third verse says that trying to figure out God only makes us realize how mentally feeble we really are. He admits that storms and disasters might lead us to believe that God is mean and always wearing a frown, when just the opposite is true. God is a God of love and grace.

Even though Job suffered terribly and experienced deep

despondency, he never gave up on God or His grace. Even though he asked some questions that would make us think that he wanted to die—he never gave up. He never sinned against God by blaming God. He did not curse God and die. He did not try to end his life. He hung in there. He maintained his integrity to the end.

A Diamond in a Garbage Dump

In Jerusalem, there is a Holocaust Museum dedicated to the memory of the millions of Jews exterminated by the Nazis in World War II. I've been there several times, and it's a depressing experience to see the horrible pictures and hear the accounts of the ghettos and the concentration camps. However, in the midst of that garbage dump of suffering, there is one glittering diamond—the story of Rachel and how God can transform horror into hope.

In one of the German concentration camps, there was a young lady named Rachel. She endured great hardship, being forced to work in the snow wearing thread-bare clothing. She witnessed many of her friends and family members being killed. One day, the guards left unexpectedly. She didn't know that the war was over until some American soldiers arrived to set the prisoners free later that day. One young American soldier told Rachel that he had come to rescue her and instructed her to gather her few possessions. Then he held the door for her and said, "After you, ma'am." Rachel started to cry. Concerned, he asked, "What's wrong, ma'am?"

She said, "I can't remember the last time someone held a door open for me. It's the nicest thing anyone has done for me in a long, long time." Rachel's words touched the soldier's heart. He stayed in contact with her after she relocated, and they became friends. Later, they fell in love and married. Only God's amazing grace can introduce a husband and wife in a setting of such horror and suffering. That's what God can do. He can take the most terrible situation imaginable and make something beautiful out of it.

So, back to the question. Would you be better off dead? In the latter years of his life, I suspect that Job must have reflected on that same question. He may have said to himself, "I thought I'd be better off dead, but now I'm glad I trusted God. If I hadn't, I would have missed out on all the blessings God has given me since then." Even though you may sometimes think that you'd be better off dead, don't give up. God is in control. The time will come for Him to take you home. However, it will be on His terms and in His timing.

Getting By with a Little Help from Your Friends

If you ask most people to tell you the story of Job, they'll probably recall a wealthy man who lost everything. Most of them can also tell you that, in the end, Job regained more than he lost. However, few people understand or appreciate the interaction between Job and his friends—which is the subject of this next chapter. Although the conversation between Job's would-be friends consumes about 80% of the text, most people can't call any of them by name. We've all had friends like them, however. They come to Job claiming to be his friends and try to help him deal with his grief. Instead of helping him, their accusations and judgments only add to Job's misery. Ever been there?

"It is better to suffer wrong than to do it, and happier to be sometimes cheated than not to trust."

– Samuel Johnson

CHAPTER 5

With Friends Like These, Who Needs Enemies?

When I was in high school, I played all the sports my school offered, but my favorite was basketball. I probably liked it best because basketball puts you closer to the crowd than football or baseball. However, being so close to the crowd could work in your favor or against you. Whenever an opposing player committed a foul, the home crowd would point their fingers at the offending player and chant in unison, "You! You! You! You! You!" It was unnerving to say the least.

I don't know if that was just an example of low-class Alabama sportsmanship. All I know is that when I was a visiting player and had a foul called on me, it wasn't a pleasant experience to have several hundred rowdy fans pointing their fingers at me and shouting, "You! You! You! You! You!" When it happened, I found myself torn between crawling under the bleachers or climbing up in them to attack those who were attacking me. That's what the three friends of Job did. Instead of empathizing with Job in his suffering, they basically pointed their self-righteous fingers and chanted, "You! You! You! You! You!" With friends like that, who needs enemies? Let's meet Job's trio of erstwhile friends in Job 2:11–13:

> *When Job's three friends, Eliphaz the Temanite, Bildad the Shuhite, and Zophar the Naamathite, heard about all the troubles that had come upon him, they set out from*

*their homes and met together by agreement
to go and sympathize with him and comfort
him. When they saw him from a distance,
they could hardly recognize him; they began
to weep aloud, and they tore their robes and
sprinkled dust on their heads. Then they sat on
the ground with him for seven days and seven
nights. No one said a word to him, because
they saw how great his suffering was.*

If that was all we ever knew about these three friends,
they would have been heroes. However, when they started
talking, they turned from heroes to zeroes! I won't take time
to examine every word they spoke. I can summarize several
chapters' worth of their remarks in one sentence: "Job, you are
suffering because you are no good."

An analytical study of the text reveals that their speeches
follow a pattern: Eliphaz speaks first, indicating that he's
probably the oldest. Then Job responds to Eliphaz. Then Bildad
speaks second, and Job responds. Finally, Zophar speaks,
followed by Job's response. This cycle repeats itself three full
times and with each cycle, they show us both the wrong way
and the right way to help a friend who's suffering.

The Wrong Way to Help Hurting Friends

Much of what Job's friends said was theologically correct, but
they made two fundamental mistakes. If you're trying to help
hurting friends, you must avoid these same errors, too.

Making False Assumptions about Why Your Friends Are Suffering

False assumptions always lead to false conclusions, and false
conclusions lead to wrong actions. Job's friends assumed that
only bad people suffer. Since Job was suffering, they concluded
that he was hiding some deep, dark sin. Instead of helping him,
their words only added to his misery.

48

Eliphaz is the first to suggest to Job: *"Is not your wickedness great? Are not your sins endless? You demanded security from your brothers for no reason; you stripped men of their clothing, leaving them naked...You sent widows away empty-handed and broke the strength of the fatherless. That is why snares are all around you, why sudden peril terrifies you, why it is so dark you cannot see, and why a flood of water covers you"* (Job 22:5– 6;9–10). There is no evidence that Job did any of those things. In fact, in the first part of the book God observes that Job was a man who was blameless and upright—a man who shunned evil. When you are trying to help friends who are hurting, be careful that you don't make the same mistake of assuming that they did something terrible to deserve their suffering.

Making Faulty Assertions about God's Will
A few years ago when hurricane Katrina devastated New Orleans, there was a church in my city whose display sign read: "The Big Easy is the Modern Sodom and Gomorrah." The message on that sign generated national exposure in the media, especially when the pastor was eager to state that it was "God's will" to send the storm to New Orleans as punishment.

Similarly, you may recall that after 9/11 some television evangelists went on the air claiming that the terrorist attacks were God's punishment on America. They later retracted their statements. However, both these examples reveal the temptation we face to make summary pronouncements about God's will. It's a mistake to assume that all suffering is a result of God punishing a person for some specific shortcoming or sin their life.

If the Bible clearly teaches that something is God's will, then it's safe to announce it. Anything beyond that is speculation and conjecture. Bildad presumed to know God's will for Job when he said: *"Does God pervert justice? Does the Almighty pervert what is right? When your children sinned against him, he gave them over to the penalty of their sin. But if you will look to God and plead with the Almighty, if you are pure and upright, even now he will rouse himself on your behalf and restore you to your rightful place"* (Job 8:3–6). Bildad claimed to be speaking for God when he told Job the reason his children died was because they were sinners. If Job repented, maybe God would restore him. We're on dangerous ground when we make the false assertion about God's will in someone else's life.

Have You Heard of the Four Spiritual Flaws?

Most Christians have heard of the "Four Spiritual Laws" from Campus Crusade. Pastor Charles Swindoll has listed what he calls, "The Four Spiritual Flaws"—four faulty assumptions that people make about suffering. (1) "If you're a Christian, you will never suffer." Instead, God's Word predicts that if you follow Jesus you will suffer. (2) "Every problem you have is answered in the Bible." The Bible addresses many problems, but if your personal computer crashes, don't look in your Bible, call technical support. (3) "If you're having problems, you are unspiritual." That was the mistake Job's friends made about tracing the source of Job's pain. (4) "God administers justice immediately." While it's true that God will one day administer perfect justice against the wicked, He doesn't always punish sin in this life. The Bible says in 1 Timothy 5:24, *"The sins of some men are obvious, reaching the place of judgment before them; the sins of others trail behind."* Don't swallow these four spiritual flaws, only to regurgitate them to a hurting friend later under the guise of being "helpful." There are better ways to help those who are hurting.

The Best Ways to Help Hurting Friends

We read in Job 2:11–13 that Job's friends started out doing the right thing. They cried with Job. They put on sackcloth and ashes and sat with him for seven days without saying anything. They could have left and gone home and remained great friends. However, when they started talking, they stopped helping. There are several things you can do if you want to help your grieving friends.

50

Be There for Them

The best thing you can do is just be with your friends during their time of suffering. You don't have to talk to them; just be there. Offer them the gift of your presence and your sincere concern. In his book, *Postmodern Pilgrims*, Len Sweet shares a letter from a physician that conveys the power of being with others in their pain. He wrote, "Today I visited an eight-year-old girl dying of cancer. She was in almost constant pain. As I entered her room, I was overcome immediately by her suffering—so unjust, unfair, and unreasonable. Even more overpowering was the presence of her grandmother lying in bed beside her with her huge body embracing this precious, inhuman suffering. I stood in awe, for I knew I was on holy ground. I will never forget the great, gentle arms and body of this grandmother. She never spoke while I was there. She was holding and participating in suffering that she could not relieve, and somehow her silent presence was relieving it. No words could express the magnitude of her love."[7]

Cry with Them

Remember Job's friends started out well: sitting with him and letting him know he wasn't alone. The Bible says, *"Rejoice with those who rejoice; weep with those who weep"* (Romans 12:15). Tears communicate your compassion much more eloquently than words ever can. Don't ever tell a hurting friend to stop crying. Instead, cry with them.

Listen More Than You Talk

In James 1:19, the Bible says that we should be *"slow to speak and quick to listen."* That's why God gave you two ears and only one mouth. He wants you to listen at least twice as much as you talk.

We've all heard that a dog is man's best friend. I think that's because you can talk to a dog and it won't talk back! Someone has said that you can keep silent and people will only suspect that you're a fool, or you can speak and remove all doubt! Every hurting person needs a friend who will listen to him or her.

Attend to Their Physical Needs

I grew up as a member of a Baptist church, and it's almost comical to think about how much food church members would deliver to families going through grief. They turned an ordinary kitchen into a warehouse of fried chicken and potato salad in a home that had experienced a death.

I once heard about three kids in school who were explaining the various symbols of their religions to their classmates. A Jewish boy showed the students a Star of David. The Catholic boy showed them a crucifix. Not to be outdone, the little Baptist boy showed them a casserole dish! We can express love in a number of ways, and simply taking food to a home of a bereaved family certainly counts.

The Bible says in Proverbs 17:17, *"There is a friend who sticks closer than a brother."* When you have friends who are suffering, be sensitive to their physical needs. People steeped in the grieving process will usually neglect to take care of their simple physical requirements. They may forget to eat, sleep, or take care of themselves. One of the finest Christian men I knew in a former church performed a unique ministry to every family that experienced a death. He would take his shoeshine kit into the home and quietly polish the shoes of the family members who would be attending the funeral. What a practical demonstration of showing love during a tough time!

Pray with Them

Prayer is always a good thing to do. However, when you pray for someone who's hurting, avoid the temptation of preaching a sermon in your prayer. Don't drone on with long, flowery prayers. Just hold hands and ask God to give your friend strength and peace.

There is a wonderful article written by Linda Mae Richardson entitled, "When I Was Diagnosed with Cancer."[8]

She wrote about the way she felt around seven different friends after they discovered she had cancer. Friend #1 said, "I can't believe you have cancer. I always thought you were so active and healthy." When that friend left, Linda wrote, "I felt alienated and somehow very 'different.'" As she talked about her different treatment options, Friend #2 said, "Whatever you do, don't take chemotherapy. It's a poison!" When she left, Linda wrote, "I felt scared and confused." Friend #3 said, "Perhaps God is disciplining you for some sin in your life." When she left, Linda wrote, "I felt guilty." Friend #4 said, "All things work together for good." When she left, Linda wrote, "I felt angry." Friend #5 said, "If your faith is great enough, God will heal you." Linda wrote, "I felt my faith must be inadequate." Friend #6 never came to visit her at all. Linda wrote about that friend, "I felt sad and alone." Friend #7 said, "I'm here. I care. I'm here to help you through this. Let me pray for you." Linda said, "When she left, I felt loved!" May we all be like that last friend!

What Can You Do When Friends Fail You?
Sometimes we play the helping role of Job's three friends. And sometimes we're the ones who are hurting. Let's put ourselves in Job's sandals for a moment. How do you think he must have felt? Maybe you're the one who's struggling, but you feel that your friends have failed you. How do you respond to that disappointment?

Don't Deny Your Disappointment
The easiest response is just to forget it and pretend it never happened. However, because these were friends of Job, he wasn't about to let them get away with their false accusations. He refused to put on a smiley face and pretend everything was fine. Nor did Job stomp off in a huff, calling over a cold shoulder, "You're not my friends anymore." Instead, he challenged their accusations. *"If I say, 'I will forget my complaint, I will change my expression, and smile.' I still dread all my sufferings, for I*

53

know you will not hold me innocent. Since I am already found guilty, why should I struggle in vain?" (Job 9:27–29). *"You smear me with lies; you are worthless physicians, all of you! If only you would be altogether silent!"* (Job 13:4–5). It's okay to be honest. If friends have failed you, let them know you are disappointed, and tell them how much you need their help.

Don't Become Bitter

When we feel that we've been mistreated, it's easy to become bitter—even in the church. Perhaps I should say, "Especially in the church." That's the reason so many churches divide into splinter groups. One person or group has been disappointed by the behavior of other Christians. This causes them to become bitter, so they either become a church drop-out, or they leave and form another church. In a stretch of several hundred yards along a highway in Elmore County, Alabama, the names of three churches tell a bitter story. First, there's an older church named "Harmony Baptist Church." However, apparently there wasn't a great deal of harmony because not far away is another church that boasts the name, "New Harmony Baptist Church." Not far from that church you can find, "Greater Harmony Baptist Church."

So often we're like the man who was stranded on a deserted island for ten years. He was the only one on the island, but there was plenty of food and water. Finally he was rescued. As his rescuers arrived, they saw three buildings he'd built on the island. When they asked him what they were, he said, "The first one is my house. The second one is my church." Puzzled, they then asked, "What about the third building?" He said, "Oh, that's the church I used to go to!"

Job was the target of hostility from his friends, but he refused to direct hostility back toward them. When someone insults us, our human nature screams out, "Yeah? Well, the same to you and more of it!" Job refused to give in to bitterness. Although he let his friends know that their helpful advice was crossing the line. *"Miserable counselors are you all! Will your*

*long winded speeches never end? What ails you that you keep
on arguing? I also could speak like you, if you were in my
place; I could make fine speeches against you and shake my
head at you. But my mouth would encourage you; comfort from
my lips would bring you relief"* (Job 12:2–3). He said, "I'm not
going to treat you the way you treated me. I'm going to treat
you the way I want to be treated."

Pray for Them
I give the same advice to those who are trying to help their
loved ones that I give to the loved ones who are hurting: pray
for each other. If you're hurting, pray for your friends who try
to help, even when their "helpfulness" is no longer helpful. I'll
develop this thought at length in a later chapter, but for now
notice that the turning point in Job's life came when he prayed
for his friends, despite his disappointment in them. In Job 42:10
we read, *"After Job had prayed for his friends, the Lord made
him prosperous again and gave him twice as much as he had
before."* Job could have easily said, "Get out of here! You're no
longer my friends." Instead, he prayed for them, and the Bible
says *after* he prayed for them, the Lord prospered him.

Is there someone from your past who failed you during your time
of pain? Don't become bitter; pray for him or her. On the night
before Jesus was crucified, He knew that one of His friends would
betray Him and another would deny Him. He knew that all of them
would desert Him in His time of need. Knowing all this, what did
He do? In the Garden of Gethsemane, He prayed for them.

Even Those We Love Will Sometimes Disappoint Us
Job's wife told him to curse God and die. His friends accused
him of wickedness. You need to know that sometimes your
friends and family members will fail you. In his book, *God's
Outrageous Claims*, Lee Stroble relates the story of a couple
on the East Coast who received a phone call from their son who
had been fighting during the Korean War.[9]

His parents hadn't heard from him in months, so they were thrilled to hear his voice. He told them he was in San Francisco on the way home. He said, "Mom, I just wanted to let you know that I'm bringing a buddy home with me. He got hurt pretty bad. He only has one eye, one arm, and one leg. I'd sure like for him to live with us." His mother said, "Sure son. He can live with us for awhile." The son insisted, "Mom, you don't understand. I want him to *live* with us." She said, "We could try it for a few months." He said, "No, Mom, he doesn't have anywhere else to go. I want him to live with us permanently. He's messed up pretty badly." After talking with her husband, she said, "Now, son, we can try it for six months or so. You're being emotional because you've been in the war. That boy will be a drag on you and a constant problem for all of us. Be reasonable." The phone clicked dead. The next day, the parents got a telegram saying their son had committed suicide. When they received his body, their tear-stained eyes looked down with unspeakable horror at the body of their son...who had lost and eye, an arm, and a leg in battle.

Jesus Is Your Best Friend
Family members and friends may fail you, but Jesus never will. Job discovered that sometimes your loved one will disappoint you and tell you to curse God and die. He found out that those we consider our closest friends may sometimes turn against us. In spite of being disappointed, Job also learned something eternally important. He learned there is Someone who will never desert you: a Redeemer and Friend who will never leave you or forsake you. In Job 19:25 he said, *"I know that my Redeemer lives, and that in the end he will stand upon the earth."* Jesus called His disciples His friends—even though they failed Him. In Matthew 11:19, Jesus is called the friend of sinners. If you need a friend right now, feel free to pray this prayer:

"Dear Lord, I need a friend who will never fail me. I need You to come into my life and to help me through

*my pain. Lord, help me not to become bitter or angry
toward those people in my life who have failed me. I
pray for them today. Because You have forgiven me,
I forgive them. Help me, Lord, to find those who are
in need. I want to be the kind of friend to them that
You are to me. In Jesus' name, Amen."*

Sleepless Nights

In 1961, Bobby Lewis sang "Tossin' and Turnin'" and put
insomnia at the top of the music charts across America. In
our stressful society, we can all relate to sleepless nights. Job,
too, suffered from insomnia. If you've ever lost a night's sleep
worrying about something, then this next chapter is for you.
Job is a case study for dealing with the kind of anxiety that
keeps us tossin' and turnin'.

"If you are distressed by anything external, the pain is not due to the thing itself, but to your estimate of it; and this you have the power to revoke at any moment."

−*Marcus Aurelius*

CHAPTER 6

When Sleep Won't Come

Have you ever had trouble sleeping at night? If so, you aren't alone. According to the Merck Medical Manual, 50% of Americans struggle with occasional insomnia, and nearly 40 million suffer from chronic insomnia. Our bodies need sleep to recharge. Without it, we accumulate a dangerous burden of sleep deficit which is why having a good night's sleep is critical for our mental and emotional well being as well.

Why Job Could Not Sleep

Here's how Job described his sleepless frustration:

> *Does not man have hard service on earth? Are not his days like those of a hired man? Like a slave longing for the evening shadows, or a hired man waiting eagerly for his wages, so I have been allotted months of futility, and nights of misery have been assigned to me. When I lie down I think, "How long before I get up?" The night drags on, and I toss 'till dawn. My body is clothed with worms and scabs, my skin is broken and festering. My days are swifter than a weaver's shuttle, and they come to an end without hope.* (Job 7:1–6)

Can you relate to that? Have you ever spent such a restless

night that you look at the clock at 3:15, then roll over and think about twenty minutes have passed only to glance again and see that it's *still* 3:15? When you understand the depth of Job's loss and suffering, you can understand why sleep wouldn't come. Four thousand years later, people are still losing sleep for these same reasons. In essence, Job was saying:

1) Life Is Hard: "I can't turn off my mind!"
In v1 Job complains, *"Does not man have hard service on earth?"* You may have seen the bumper sticker with a similar sentiment: "Life is hard. Then you die." One hundred years ago, Americans got an average of 10 hours sleep a night. Today the average is closer to seven hours a night. We are suffering from a variety of health issues because we aren't getting enough sleep. Women are 10% more likely to suffer from insomnia than men.

According to the Merck Medical Manual, "There are several types of insomnia. Difficulty falling asleep, called sleep-onset insomnia, often occurs when people cannot let their minds relax and they continue to think and worry. Difficulty staying asleep, called sleep maintenance insomnia, is more common among older people than among younger people. People with this type of insomnia fall asleep normally but wake up several hours later and cannot fall asleep again easily. Sometimes they drift in and out of a restless, unsatisfactory sleep. Early morning awakening, another type of insomnia, may be a sign of depression in people of any age."

The human brain is an amazing instrument. It starts working the moment you're born and doesn't stop working until you stand up in front of a crowd to speak! Seriously, your mind doesn't stop—even when you're asleep. Your mind is still at work, which is why we have dreams. Wouldn't it be great if you could find an "on/off switch" in your brain? Then when you got ready to sleep, you could just flip the switch!

2) Life Is Boring: "I can't get out of a rut!"

In v2 Job said, *"Like a slave longing for the evening shadows, or a hired man waiting eagerly for his wages, so I have been allotted months of futility."* Job compares his life to that of a slave who goes to work and does the same mindless thing day after day. He longs for the day to be over. His life has degenerated into a boring rut. Psychologist Rollo May has written: "The clearest picture of an empty life is the man who gets up at the same hour every weekday morning, goes to work, performs the same tasks at the office, lunches at the same places, leaves the same tip for the waitress, comes home and watches the same TV shows each night; He spends a two week vacation at the same place every summer which he does not enjoy. He goes to church but does not really know why he goes, and moves through a routine, mechanical existence year after year until he finally retires at age 65 and very soon thereafter dies of heart failure, possibly brought on by repressed anger. Though I always suspect he died from boredom." You may be in a vocational rut or a financial rut, digging yourself a deeper rut. On the other hand, you may find yourself in a spiritual rut where you show up at church and expect to get some kind of spiritual booster shot to carry you through the week. Remember, a rut is nothing but a grave with both ends kicked out.

3) Life Is Fragile: "I can't ignore my pain!"

If you've ever been severely ill, you know how fragile life can be. In v5 Job said, *"My body is clothed with worms and scabs, my skin is broken and festering."* Satan had attacked Job's health. He had covered his skin with boils and open, oozing sores. Job couldn't sleep because he just couldn't get comfortable at night. As you get older, you realize how fragile your health is. Those of us who struggle with chronic back pain know what it is to try to find a sleep position that seems to cause the least amount of back pain. That's another cause of sleeplessness.

61

4) *Life Is Frustrating: "I can't stop worrying!"*

In v6 Job said, *"My days are swifter than a weaver's shuttle, and they come to an end without hope."* Job had already spoken about months of futility, and now he compares his days to a weaver's shuttle. In Bible times, weavers made cloth by stretching threads lengthwise on a wooden loom called a warp. Then a weaver would load a long wooden pole with threads (called the weft) that allowed accomplished weavers to interlace the threads with great speed. A wooden "shuttle" would slide back and forth making a loud clacking sound. As Job considered his personal frustration, he observed that his life was mostly noise and motion like that shuttle. He also says that life will come to an end without hope, referring to the brevity of life. As a young pastor, I remember visiting a man in his 90s who was residing in a nursing home. He was in poor health physically, but his mind was sharp. He made a statement about life that I've never forgotten. He said, "My years rush by, but the days drag by." Worry and anxiety will keep you awake at night. Anxiety is the gnawing dread in your gut that something bad may happen. In Job 30:27, Job said, *"The churning inside me never stops; days of suffering confront me."*

How Can I Find Peace to Sleep Soundly?

We've all heard the expression: "sleep like a baby" (usually said by someone who never had a newborn infant in their home!). A few years ago, Oklahoma University football coach Bob Stoops lost the national championship to USC in the Orange Bowl. Oklahoma was outmatched and their opponents trounced them. A few days after the game, a sportswriter asked Coach Stoops how he slept the night after his team was embarrassed. He said, "I slept like a baby. I'd sleep a few minutes...wake up and cry...sleep a few more minutes...wake up and cry ..."

Job wasn't sleeping, he was crying out to God—his eyes red from weeping. *"What is man that you make so much of him, that you give him so much attention, that you examine him every morning and test him every moment? Will you never look*

*away from me, or let me alone even for an instant? If I have
sinned, what have I done to you, O watcher of men? Why have
you made me your target? Have I become a burden to you?"*
(Job 7:17–20). If you're having trouble sleeping, you'll find a
variety of sleep-aid products available. Some people try pills.
Some people try alcohol. Some people try sleep machines that
make white noise or the sounds of surf breaking on the sea. A
few years ago, I bought a sound machine that was supposed
to make the sound of rain falling. Instead, it reminded me of
bacon frying, which made me want to get up and eat!

Actually, I've found that the older I get, the less sleep I
get. Most nights I'm in bed before 11:00, and I wake up around
five the next morning. However, there are some nights when I
wake up, look over at the digital clock, and see that it's around
3:00—too early to get up. There are two things that I do to help
me go back to sleep—the same things that Job did when he
was fighting insomnia. I use that time to pray and to mentally
recite Bible verses. So if you're suffering from the insomnia of
despair, try these two all-natural sleep-aid methods.

Speak to God Honestly

If you think Job endured his suffering silently and patiently,
think again. We speak of the "patience of Job." However, he
didn't demonstrate much patience at the beginning. At this
stage, he complained bitterly to God. In v11 he said, *"I will
not keep silent; I will speak out in the anguish of my spirit, I
will complain in the bitterness of my soul."* Job later became
a patient man because tribulation produces patience. However,
in the middle of the night when he couldn't sleep, Job uttered
some strong complaints to the Lord.

You need to know that you can speak honestly to God.
You aren't going to surprise Him or even offend Him. So when
you're struggling to sleep at night, express your true feelings
in prayer to the Lord. However, as you express your deepest
feelings to God, don't forget to thank Him and praise Him
as well. There's a one-sentence prayer that David prayed in

Psalm 4 that you could call the "sleep soundly prayer." It says, *"I will lie down and sleep in peace, for you alone, O Lord, make me dwell in safety"* (Psalm 4:8). You ought to write that prayer down and memorize it. When you find yourself afraid or worrying, just keep repeating that prayer to God.

When most of us were kids we learned a little bedside prayer that said:

> "Now I lay me down to sleep,
> I pray the Lord my soul to keep.
> If I should die before I wake.
> I pray the Lord my soul to take."

I've always been a little troubled by that prayer. It plants the scary idea into the mind of children that they could die while they're sleeping—not a very comforting thought! I recently read a revised version of the prayer that focuses more on God's care throughout the night and on waking up the next morning. It says:

> "Now I lay me down to sleep.
> My faith in God, it runs so deep.
> That if I should die, before I wake,
> I trust my Lord my soul to take.
> Until that time, till death does come,
> He'll wake me with the morning sun.
> The birds will sing, and I will cheer,
> That God is good, and I'm still here!"

So, if you find yourself unable to sleep, try praying. Talk to God honestly. Pray for your family members and friends. Pray for your nation and your president. When I pray in bed, I usually fall asleep before I can pray for everyone who comes to mind.

Listen to God Intently through His Word

In the final chapters of Job, God is going to speak clearly to Job. If Job had been listening to God earlier, he might have avoided some sleepless nights. Instead of tossing and turning in your bed at night when you can't sleep, you can pray. And there's something else you can do: listen to God's voice. He may speak into your spirit with a still small voice, like He did to Elijah in a cave. However, God speaks most often and most clearly through His Word, the Bible.

When I have trouble sleeping at night, I will often begin to quote silently as many scriptures as I can recall. I usually start by quoting Isaiah 26:3: *"You will keep in perfect peace him whose mind is steadfast because he trusts in you."* Then I go with a slow recollection of the 23rd Psalm emphasizing the personal pronouns and trying to envision the settings. "The Lord is MY shepherd, I shall not want. He makes ME lie down in green pastures; He leads ME beside the still waters." Sometimes I don't even make it to the last verse before I'm asleep! The Word of God has a calming effect on God's children.

God's Prescription for Insomnia

You may be thinking, "I wish God would speak to me!" He already has. He has made precious and certain promises to you in His Word. God is speaking, are you listening? Are you reading and claiming the promises of His Word? Remember the reasons I listed above why we sometimes can't sleep? Here's God's prescription for those primary causes of insomnia.

When Life Is Hard...

Jesus says: *"Take my yoke upon you and learn of me...for my yoke is easy and my burden is light"* (Matthew 11:30). When life is hard, we often become weary and heavy laden. A yoke was a harness that two oxen could share together to pull a load. When you accept the yoke of Jesus, His strength is so great that the yoke becomes easy and the burden of life becomes light. You can't deal with all the demands that life throws your way without having the strength of Christ in your life.

When You're in a Rut...

Jesus says: *"So if the Son sets you free, you will be free indeed!"* (John 8:36). Jesus can set you free from the penalty of sin, but He also sets you free from the boredom of life. For someone who doesn't know Christ, this life is all there is. However, for those of us who follow Jesus, we're part of a great adventure that starts here and will continue for all eternity. When you know Jesus, and He sets you free, you can wake up every morning with a sense of excitement and purpose for your life. Jesus sets you free from living in a rut.

When You're in Pain...

God says: *"My grace is sufficient for you, for my power is made perfect in weakness"* (2 Corinthians 12:9). When Paul struggled to deal with his thorn in the flesh, he asked the Lord to remove it, but God didn't take away the pain. Instead God promised that His grace would sustain him through the pain. Of course, when you're hurting, you naturally want God to take away the pain. He may heal you, or He may assure you that His love, mercy, and grace will be powerful enough to carry you through your suffering.

When You Worry...

The Bible says: *"Cast all your anxiety on him because he cares for you"* (1 Peter 5:7). One of my favorite stories is about a chronic worrier who made everybody at work miserable. He was always frowning, moaning, and groaning about the worst that could happen. However, one day, he came to work with a smile on his face and a spring in his step. One of his coworkers noticed the change and said, "Man, what's different about you? You used to worry about everything, and now you act as if you didn't have a care in the world." The former worry-wart said, "I discovered the best way to get rid of worry. I have hired a man who does all my worrying for me. That's all he does." The coworker said, "That sounds great. How much do you have to pay him to worry for you?" The man said, "I pay him $10,000 a month." His coworker was astonished and said, "But you don't make that much money. How are you going to pay for him?" The worry-wart just smiled and said, "That's not my worry—it's his!"

Wouldn't it be great if you could find someone who would take all your worries away? You do. The Bible says we can cast all our cares on the Lord. Psalm 121:4 says, *"He who watches over Israel will neither slumber nor sleep."* If you find yourself unable to sleep because you're worrying about something, the Lord says to you, "There's no sense in both of us staying awake about this. I'm not going to be sleeping tonight, why don't you just give me your cares, and you go on to sleep."

Peace in the Midst of the Storm
One of my favorite episodes from the life of Jesus was when He and His disciples were in a boat at night, crossing the Sea of Galilee. Matthew 8:24 describes the scene: *"A furious storm came up on the lake so that the waves swept over the boat. But Jesus was sleeping."* Did you catch that point? The winds howled, lightning flashed, and the thunder rumbled, but Jesus slept. The disciples, terrified by the storm, woke Jesus up and said, "Lord, save us! We're going to drown!" Jesus opened his eyes and simply said, "You of little faith, why are you so afraid?" Then He rebuked the storm and said, "Peace, be still." The Bible says that immediately it was completely calm.

That story has given me great peace because I've learned several personal applications for my life. First, because Jesus is in my "boat" (my life), that doesn't mean I won't encounter storms. I can expect them to happen, so they no longer catch me off guard. Second, if Jesus is in my life, I shouldn't fear or worry about the storms of life. Meaning, if He can sleep through them, I can survive them, too. Finally, in the midst of my darkest nights and fiercest storms, Jesus can speak peace into my stormy soul. I've learned that sometimes He calms the storms, but most often He calms the hearts of those in the storm. So, if sleep won't come because of fears and worries, you can certainly relate to Job. Nevertheless, there is hope and healing for your insomnia through the One who calms the storms.

Take Me out to the Ballgame

In the middle of a book about Job, you might be surprised to find my next chapter title on baseball umpires. However, there is a unique Hebrew word found in Job 9—the only place where it's used in the Bible. Our best English word that captures its true meaning is "umpire." In this next chapter, we'll discover how God's umpire can help us find peace in the middle of our pain.

"He jests at scars that never felt a wound."

—William Shakespeare

CHAPTER 7

God's
Umpire

∂∾⋖∽

Although the story of Job happened centuries before Jesus was born in Bethlehem, God sprinkled plenty of prophetic clues about Him in the Old Testament. In the middle of Job's story, God hid in plain sight a powerful picture of the mediating work of Christ. So for the next few pages, let's take a short break from the story of Job and take a look at the larger story of God's salvation.

If you're familiar with America's national pastime, then you've probably heard (or shouted yourself), "Kill the ump!" That phrase probably originated from Ernest Lawrence Thayer's classic poem, "Casey at the Bat" written in 1888. It's a long ballad about a baseball game between two local teams where Casey carries the final hope of the team from Mudville and the fans blame the umpire for his strike out. While most of us think of an umpire as someone who calls balls and strikes at a baseball game, the meaning of the word goes beyond the baseball diamond. The definition of an umpire is "A person appointed to settle a dispute that individuals or parties have been unable to resolve; an arbitrator."[10]

In Job 9:32–35, Job expresses his frustration at not being able to talk to God as an equal. He cries out for a mediator—an umpire. He says, *"He [God] is not a man like me that I might answer him, that we might confront each other in court. If only there were someone to arbitrate between us, to lay his hand upon us both, someone to remove God's rod from me, so that his terror would frighten me no more. Then I would speak up without fear of him, but as it now stands with me, I cannot."*

Our Problem: We Desperately Need a Spiritual Umpire

The New American Standard Version of this passage in Job 9 says: "There is no umpire between us, who may lay his hand upon us both." In the midst of his pain, Job cried out for an umpire to mediate the disagreements he had with his Creator. As Job searched for answers, he made three observations:

"God Isn't Like Me"

Job recognized that God was not human like him. There are at least two fundamental distinctions between God and me. God is eternal, and I am a finite creature. The other difference is that God is holy (perfect), and I am a sinner. God has such an aversion to sin that the Bible says that He cannot look at evil. The prophet Habakkuk wrote, *"Oh, God, are you not from everlasting? Your eyes are too pure to look on evil; you cannot tolerate wrong"* (Habakkuk 1:12–13).

"My Sins Separate Me from God"

The second part of our problem is that our sins have broken our relationship with God. When God created Adam and Eve in the Garden of Eden, their souls were pure and undefiled. They could walk with God and talk with Him in the cool of the evening. However, when sin entered their lives, it destroyed that precious intimacy. The Bible says, *"Your iniquities have separated you from your God; your sins have hidden his face from you"* (Isaiah 59:2).

"I Can't Relate to God without a Qualified Mediator"

In the midst of his pain and suffering, Job cried out that he needed a neutral third party to lay one hand on God and the other hand on him to resolve their conflict. He needed someone to negotiate with God so that He would withdraw His rod of punishment. He needed an umpire—a mediator.

Some people think that they have no need of a spiritual mediator. They make the faulty assumption that they can relate to their concept of God on their own. However, those of us who have committed one sinful deed, or had a single sinful thought, have been disqualified from serving as our own mediator with God. Rarely, in the American justice system an accused person chooses to serve as his or her own attorney. Our laws permit that privilege. However, I've heard lawyers say, "The person who serves as his own attorney has a fool for a client." That's what Job recognized. We all need someone to arbitrate between us and God.

God's Provision: He Has Given Us a Spiritual Umpire

Job expressed the same spiritual challenge that we all face. How can we, as sinful creatures, relate to a holy, perfect God? Thankfully, God has already provided the solution. Someone has observed that religion is man reaching out for God, but Christianity is God reaching out to man. God reached out to us in the person of Jesus Christ.

Jesus Christ is our umpire—our spiritual mediator. He bridges the chasm between sinful man and holy God. The Bible says: *"For there is one God and one mediator between God and men, the man Christ Jesus who gave himself as a ransom for all men"* (1 Timothy 2:5–6). Surveys have revealed that Americans have more interest in spiritual matters than ever before. However, a growing number of people seek to relate to God using their own personal methods. They see no need for Jesus as a mediator.

Sarah Michelle Gellar is a well-known television and movie star. She starred in a show called Buffy the Vampire Killer and other teen flicks. When asked about God, she expressed the position of many of confused young people. She said: "I consider myself a spiritual person. I believe in an idea of God, although it's my own personal ideal. I find most religions interesting, and I've been to every kind of denomination: Catholic, Christian, Jewish, Buddhist. I've taken bits from everything and customized it."[11]

However, the Bible teaches that Jesus is the only reliable mediator between God and man. In addition, there are two important aspects of Jesus' role as our spiritual umpire.

Jesus Is the Exclusive Mediator

First Timothy 2:5 makes it clear that there is *"one God and one mediator."* When someone owns "exclusive rights," it means that nobody else qualifies. Jesus is the *exclusive* mediator because He claimed to be the *only* way to God. Jesus is not the *best* way to heaven—He is the *only* way. That's not a popular statement in today's culture of plurality and tolerance. Today, the politically correct position is that there are many pathways to God: the Buddhist pathway, the Hindu pathway, the Muslim pathway, the Christian pathway, and many others. Nevertheless, to accept religious pluralism is to deny the exclusive claims of Jesus.

Jesus said, *"I am the way, and the truth and the life. No one comes to the Father except through me"* (John 14:6). According to Jesus' own words, He is the exclusive mediator between God and man. You don't have to be a simpleton to accept that. One of the most brilliant individuals of the 20th Century, C.S. Lewis, proved that. He was a renowned professor at Oxford University in England. At one time, he claimed to be an atheist and set out on a rational pursuit to disprove the claims of the Bible. After honestly search for truth, he actually became a devoted follower of Jesus. This intellectual giant affirmed that Jesus was who He claimed to be. He removed the popular option of claiming that Jesus was just one man in long line of religious teachers.

He once wrote: "The things Jesus says are different from what any other teacher has said. Others say, 'This is the truth about the Universe. This is the way you ought to go," but He says, "I AM the truth, and the Way and the Life. No man can reach absolute reality, except through Me.'"[12] He continued this train of thought: "The man who said the sort of things

Jesus said would not be simply a great moral teacher. He would either be a lunatic—on the level with a man who says he is a poached egg—or else he would be the Devil of Hell. You can shut Him up for a fool, you can spit at Him and kill Him as a demon, or you can fall at his feet and call Him Lord and God. But let us not come with any patronizing nonsense about His being a great human teacher."[13]

Jesus Is an Expensive Mediator

First Timothy 2:6 also says that Jesus *"gave himself as a ransom."* A ransom is the purchase-price of someone's freedom. In 1193, the English King Richard I, also known as Richard the Lionhearted, was returning from leading a Crusade to the Holy Land. As he returned through Europe, Leopold V. captured him in Austria. The Holy Roman Emperor demanded a ransom for Richard's release of 150,000 marks, which equated to three tons of silver. This was an enormous ransom demand. Nevertheless, the people of England so loved their king that they submitted to extra taxation, and many nobles donated their fortunes for Richard's release. After many months, the money was raised and King Richard returned to England. That's where we get the expression, "a king's ransom."

To us, the term "a king's ransom" could better be applied to the tremendous price that the King of Kings paid for our sins. This King wasn't ransomed; He willingly paid the ransom for us so we could be set free. Ours was the most expensive ransom in the history of the world. Also during the Crusades, another Englishman, Lord Grimbaldi was captured by the Saracens. The Turkish prince demanded the severed right hand of Grimbaldi's young bride, Lady Eleanor, as ransom. In a tremendous act of courage and sacrifice, Lady Eleanor complied and had her left hand amputated as ransom for her husband. That's what Jesus did for you, but He didn't just give His hand; He gave His life.

Jesus Is Available to All

First Timothy 2:6 doesn't say that Jesus gave his life as a ransom for a few. He gave His life as a ransom for everyone, even to those who refuse to accept the free gift of eternal life.

There's a modern story called, "The Parable of the Donuts and Pushups" that illustrates Jesus' willingness to pay the price for our deliverance. Once there was a professor in a Bible College named Dr. Christianson. Every year he taught a Bible Survey course that all freshmen were required to take. Although he tried to make theology interesting, he found that most students were bored.

One year he devised a new plan to explain salvation. He had a gifted student in his class named Steve. Steve was not only an excellent student, but he was a star athlete as well. One day Dr. Christianson asked him, "Steve how many push ups do you think you can do?" Steve said, "I usually do about 200 pushups a day." Dr. Christianson said, "Would you be willing to do some pushups for me in class tomorrow to illustrate salvation?" Steve said, "Sure." Then Dr. Christianson explained to Steve privately exactly what he had in mind.

The next day, when the students arrived, they saw two boxes of tantalizing donuts on Dr. Christianson's desk. The students' mouths began to water as they suspected that they might get to enjoy those donuts in class. Dr. Christianson took a box of donuts and held them out to a girl on the front row and asked, "Cynthia, would you like a donut?" She said, "Yes!" Dr. Christianson turned to Steve and said, "Steve, would you do ten pushups so Cynthia can have a donut?" Steve jumped down to the floor, did ten fast pushups and then returned to his seat. The students laughed and cheered, and the professor handed a tasty donut to Cynthia.

Dr. Christianson went to the next student and said, "Joe, would you like a donut?" When he nodded the professor said, "Steve, will you do ten more pushups so Joe can have a donut?" Steve dropped down and did another ten pushups. And so it continued. For every student who got a donut, Steve had to do ten pushups. After six or seven students received donuts, Steve was sweating and the students were no longer cheering or smiling. Dr. Christianson came to Mike, who was a member of the basketball team. Mike said, "I can do my own pushups." Dr. Christianson said, "No, that's not the way it works. Steve has to do the pushups." Mike said, "Then I don't want a donut."

Dr. Christianson shrugged and said, "Steve, please do ten pushups so Mike can have a donut." When Steve started the pushups, Mike shouted, "Hey! I said I didn't want a donut!" Dr. Christianson turned to the entire class and said, "Listen and listen well: This is my class, these are my donuts, and I get to make the plan." As he laid a donut on Mike's desk he said, "If you don't want your donut, just leave it on the desk. I won't force you to eat it."

As the professor went to each student, Steve did another ten pushups. After all the exertion, he was beginning to slow down and was sweating profusely. Soon he didn't even rise between the sets; he just stayed on the floor waiting for the next set. By now, some of the students were getting angry. They all responded no when Dr. Christianson offered them the sweet treat. The desks were covered with uneaten donuts, but still Steve was having a rough time trying to comply with the order to do pushups. His arms were shaking and he could hardly raise himself from the floor. Robert, an unbeliever, balked when Dr. Christianson asked him if he wanted a donut. He angrily replied, "You're crazy, and this is a stupid plan." As Dr. Christianson put a donut on Robert's desk he said, "Some people say that. Steve, do ten pushups so that Robert can have a donut that he doesn't want. Robert, be sure to count and make sure Steve does all ten."

Soon, the only sound in the classroom was Steve's heavy breathing and a few quiet sobs from some of the girls as they watched Steve agonize over each effort. He had to take several seconds to try to rest between each push up. By now, he had completed twenty-five sets of ten pushups. When Dr. Christianson came to the last student he said, "Susan, would you like a donut? With tears streaming down her face she said, "Can't I help Steve? He's in such agony!"

The professor was on the verge of tears himself as he said, "No, Steve has to do it alone. I looked in my grade book and Steve is the only student with a perfect A+ average. He's the only student who hasn't skipped class or missed out on turning in a paper. Steve told me that when a player makes a mistake at football practice the coach orders them to do pushups to pay for his error. So Steve and I made a deal. Since all of you have messed up in my class, Steve has agreed to do ten pushups for each of you so you can enjoy the donut." He turned to an exhausted Steve and said, "Steve, do ten more pushups for Susan to have a donut." One, two, three, four... five...six ...seven...eight...nine...ten. As Steve strained to finish that final pushup, he realized that he had accomplished all that was required of him. With a tired, but joy-filled voice, he said, "It is finished!" Then his weary arms finally buckled and he slid to the floor.

Dr. Christianson turned to the stunned students and said, "As so it was, that our Savior, Jesus Christ, gave His all on the cross to pay for our sins. With the understanding that He had done everything required of Him, He yielded up His life and said, 'It is finished.' And like some of the students in this room, many people leave God's gift on the desk, uneaten." As two of the guys helped Steve to his feet, the professor said, "Well, done, good and faithful servant. Class dismissed." None of those students forgot the powerful lesson they'd witnessed that day.

Have You Called for an Umpire?

Four thousand years ago, Job recognized the core problem of the human species. How can we as sinful creatures ever hope to relate to a perfect, holy God? You can't be reconciled with God without a qualified umpire who can mediate your differences. This mediator must be able to relate to human beings and to relate to God at the same time. On the basis of His humanity,

Jesus offers you one of His nailed pierced hands. Based upon His Deity, He reaches into heaven and takes the hand of His Heavenly Father. As He died on the Cross, He brought both together for the first time and cried "It is finished!" And hope was born.

Finding Hope

One of the most valuable commodities in the world is hope. Surveys have revealed that Americans are more afraid now than they were ten years ago. People fear terrorist attacks, monster storms, gas prices escalating, or worse—no gas at any price. Jesus said that in the last days people's hearts would fail because of *fear* (Luke 21:26). I think one reason people are more afraid is because we know so much more about what's happening in the world. In a world of 24-hour news and weather channels, we can turn on the TV at any hour and hear about wars, hurricanes, bird flu, or suicide bombers. That's the nature of the news—to report on the bad news. When it comes to bad news, maybe ignorance is bliss. If you could use a little good news, you'll be sure to find it in the next part of Job's story. If you're afraid, or in pain, or lonely, or suffering—there is hope—and that hope is in Jesus Christ.

*"God had one Son on earth without sin,
but never one without suffering."*

–Augustine

CHAPTER 8

Hope in the
Midst of Pain

I have never been a huge fan of professional boxing, but it was almost impossible not to be interested in the epic boxing matches between Smokin' Joe Frazier and Mohammed Ali in the 70s. In their first fight in 1971, Frazier knocked out Mohammed Ali for the victory. Then in their rematch in 1973 Ali won a 12th round decision. That set up what some boxing fans consider to be one of the greatest fights in boxing history. Ali and Frazier met on October 1, 1975 in what was called the "Thrilla in Manila." Ali, who considered himself a poet, boasted that it would be a "killa, a chilla, a thrilla when I get the gorilla in Manila." (Robert Frost's reputation is still secure!)

Nevertheless, for twelve rounds, Frazier pounded Ali into submission. Ali had been knocked to the canvas, and Frazier was clearly ahead in points. Observers believed that it was only a matter of time before Frazier knocked out Ali. Yet in the 13th round, the fight changed suddenly. Ali started to jab Frazier with his left hand repeatedly. He hit Frazier with nine straight left jabs and then followed with a right cross that knocked out Frazier's mouthpiece. From that point on, Frazier's punches lost their power. Frazier stumbled through the 14th round, and then his trainer threw in the towel when Frazier was unable to answer the bell for the next round.

That's a lot like what happened to Job. For 12 chapters, Satan had pounded, pummeled, and pressed Job. Job had been knocked down numerous times. Pow!—Job lost his fortune. Bam!—Job lost his family. Jab!—Job's wife told him to give up. Another vicious right landed when Job's friends accused him of great sin. It was sickening to hear punch after punch thrown at Job. After 12 rounds, Job was badly bruised and bleeding. The spectators, all angels in heaven, must have surely hidden their faces as the thug, the bully, the evil prince of darkness beat their beloved Job.

Suddenly, out of nowhere, Job slips a sudden uppercut through Satan's attack. Initially, it seemed to be a weak and fragile effort, almost unnoticed. But it lands squarely on Satan's chin, and suddenly, the devil staggers backward. What was the punch? It was Job's powerful affirmation in Job 13: "Though he slay me, yet will I hope in him." At this, Satan takes a verbal uppercut and stops in his tracks. With a look of unbelief in his wicked eyes, the adversary wobbles, and then falls—knocked out cold. The angels in heaven erupt with cheers, as Job stands there with his gloves raised ready to repel any more blows from his fallen foe.

Granted, Job wasn't crowned as champ until chapter 42, but from this point in the story until then, Satan was beaten. Every follower of God is in the same fight Job fought. We aren't fighting against a human foe but against an invisible, malevolent enemy. Understanding Job's fight can help make the difference between victory and defeat. These are ten words that can change your life because they change your outlook on life. These ten simple syllables can deliver a knock-out punch against our enemy. Try reading them aloud: "Though he slay me, yet will I trust in him."

The devil's chief tool to discourage God's servants is fear: fear of pain; fear of death; fear of the unknown. At the moment of intense pain, Job makes a confession that completely nullified Satan's strategy. Satan wanted to make Job so miserable that Job would curse God. However, when Job confessed, "Even if God kills me, I'm still going to hope in Him," it knocked the wind out of Satan. Have you come to a place where you can say the same thing? "Whatever happens, even if I die, I'm not giving up. My hope is in God!" Satan has no defense against that kind of testimony.

How to Have H.O.P.E.

A few years ago, I developed an acrostic for H.O.P.E. that stands for Having Only Positive Expectations. Job was a great example of a man who Had Only Positive Expectations in the midst of terrible pain. To put Job's loss in perspective, it would be like Bill Gates and Microsoft going completely under in one day—plus Job lost his precious children. Job was in a fight for his life and sanity. He was still grieving and suffering miserably. His friends were there, but they told him that God was punishing Job for some terrible secret sin in his life. In spite of all that, in Job 13:15–16 Job said: *"Though he slay me, yet will I hope in him; I will surely defend my ways to his face. Indeed, this will turn out for my deliverance, for no godless man would dare come before him!"* Job meant that he would not give up hope in God—even if God killed him. Of course, God had no intention of doing so. He was the One keeping him alive. Job was just considering what we often call the "worst-case-scenario" and decided that he was going to maintain hope whatever happened. In doing so, he showed us a two-fold balance between facing the reality of our suffering, but maintaining a positive outlook:

Job Questioned God, but Never Blamed Him

Do you ever question God? Job did. Have you ever wondered how many questions Job asked God? I personally counted Job's questions for God and discovered that he asked 114 questions—he was the Larry King of antiquity! Job was constantly asking God what He was doing and why he was suffering. Nevertheless, in the process of questioning God, Job never once blamed Him.

Scripture reports, *"In all this, Job did not sin by charging God with wrongdoing"* (Job 1:22). I've learned that when

I'm hurting, it's okay for me to question my Father. However, I have no right to demand His answers. In Job's story, God eventually replied to Job, but instead of giving answers God asked questions of His own!

Job Complained to God, but Never Cursed Him

Job didn't deny his pain and bitterness. He honestly complained about his suffering, but he never cursed God. In Job 2, when Mrs. Job suggested that he do so, Job replied, *"Shall we accept good from God and not trouble? In all this, Job did not sin what he said"* (Job 2:10). When you're struggling with pain and suffering, you don't have to stick your head in the sand and deny your pain. Job could complain against God because he knew Him and loved Him. My favorite Bible teacher, Ron Dunn, used to talk about how only those children of God who have a familiar intimacy with God can be totally honest with Him. He used to say, "Lord, I'm surprised you have as many friends as you do, the way you treat the ones you have!" That's honesty! So as you suffer, be honest, but be careful what you say and how you say it. This passage infers that we can cross the line from complaint to sinning against God. Job resisted these temptations, and so can we.

A Question Everyone Must Answer

Job's second amazing statement is in Job 14:1–2. Job observed, *"Man born of woman is full of trouble. He springs up like a flower and withers away; like a fleeting shadow, he does not endure."* This body that we live in is temporary. Like a flower, it will one day crumble and wither away. Nevertheless, Job understood that there is more to life than just the body. In Job 14:14–17, he asked one of the most profound questions in human history: *"If a man dies, will he live again?"* It's a question that every person on earth thinks about at one time or another. Is there life after death?

This question deserves our consideration because all of us are going to die. If we're honest, most of us are like the little boy who was wondering about death so he wrote a letter to God:

> *Dear God,*
> *What is it like when a person dies? Nobody*
> *will tell me. I don't want to do it...I just want*
> *to know.*
> *Your friend,*
> *Mike*

Like Mike, we all want to know. Everybody has an opinion on death. Atheists claim that death is the end of human existence and that after death there is only nothingness. Buddhists claim that a person may be reincarnated as another type of animal. Regardless of one's religion, it's a fundamental question because if there is only one life to live, and this is it, then you should grab all the marbles for yourself. However, if there is life after death, you should find out what it's like and what will happen.

This is one of the few questions that Job asked and immediately answered his own question. By faith, Job's answer was: "I will wait for my renewal." In Job 14:14–15 he said, *"All the days of my hard service I will wait for my renewal to come. You will call and I will answer you."* Job's short answer was, "Yes, there is life after death." However, some theologians aren't as definitive in their answer to this question. I remember when I was in seminary we studied a book called *Systematic Theology* written by Dr. Paul Tillich. When he was writing about the possibility of life after death he wrote: "Since Eternal Life is Life and not undifferentiated identity and since the Kingdom of God is the universal actualization of love, the element of individualization cannot be eliminated."[14] If you didn't understand that statement, don't feel alone. It represents the stuttering attempt of theologians to answer Job's simple question. It's been my experience that most theologians write books that only other theologians can understand.

In contrast, the Bible speaks simply and plainly about our hope for eternal life. A few months ago, I visited with a grieving family who had lost a teenager in an automobile accident. They were asking me about life after death and heaven. What do you think I said, to them? "Since eternal life is not undifferentiated identity, the element of actualized individualization cannot be eliminated." No. I simply told them what Jesus said. Compare His simple, profound words to those of a theologian. In John 11:25 Jesus said, *"I am the resurrection and the life. He who believes in me will live, even though he dies."* If a man dies, shall he live again? If you place your trust in Jesus as your Lord and Savior the answer to that question is a loud and clear "Yes!"

Hope from Heaven
Whenever you study the Bible, you should always ask two questions. First, what was God doing and saying back when this scripture was written? The next question you should always ask is this: What is God saying to me today? Through the story of Job, God gives us instructions for finding heavenly hope in the midst of our pain:

When you suffer, resist the temptation to turn away from God
Can you remember when you found yourself at the lowest point of your life? It might have been after a job loss or the death of someone you loved. It might have been when your parents split up or when you went through a divorce. Maybe you're at that low point right now. Like Job, you face the temptation to curse God.

Do you find yourself at a point where you want to shake your fist in God's face and say, "God, why are you allowing these terrible things to happen to me?" That's exactly how Job felt. However, like all temptation, you can resist it. Suffering is only temporary—for followers of Christ, conditions will always improve. As you think of Job's suffering, don't ever forget what happened later in his life. God restored all that he had lost and more. You've got to believe that in the end things will get better for you—if not in this life, in the next life for sure.

I love the story of the little boy who went to the pet store to pick out a new puppy. He looked down into a box of about a dozen furry puppies all clamoring over each other. There was one little puppy looking up at him wagging his tail furiously. The little boy saw that tail and said, "I want the one with the happy ending!" When you choose Jesus, you choose the life with the happy ending. Here's God's promise found in 1 Peter 5:10, *"And the God of all grace, who called you to his eternal glory in Christ, after you have suffered a little while, will himself restore you and make you strong, firm and steadfast."*

In your darkest hour, confess your hope in God

It's not enough simply to have hope; it's important to *confess* your hope. Say it out loud so you can hear yourself say it and draw strength from that confession. That's what Job did. The Bible teaches that there is enormous power in the spoken word. If you think bad thoughts and confess bad possibilities, that's generally what you'll experience. However, whenever you make a good confession based on faith, good things usually happen.

Jesus underscored the power of confession in Matthew 16. Jesus was asking the disciples who He was. They told Him, "Some say John the Baptist, others say Elijah; and still others Jeremiah, or one of the prophets." Then Jesus said, "But who do *you* say I am?" The only one to answer was Simon Peter. He said, *"'You are the Christ, the Son of the Living God.' Jesus said, 'Blessed are you Simon son of John...I tell you that you are Peter and upon this rock I will build my church and the gates of hell shall not prevail against it'"* (Matthew 16:14–19).

Jesus didn't mean he was going to build a church on Peter. He was going to build a church on the *confession* that Peter made. Whenever you make a strong confession that Jesus is the Son of the Living God, Satan and all of his demons tremble. Every confession of faith and hope is like a battering ram that slams into the gates of hell. So, go ahead, make a confession of your hope. Even if you don't feel like it, confess it anyway—you'll find a new measure of strength as a result.

You may ask, "How can I confess my hope when all I feel is pain?" One way is to believe that God is using your suffering to make you stronger. Job didn't fully understand about the agreement between God and Satan, but he knew he was being tested. Job also knew he was going to pass the test. In fact, he confessed that all suffering is a test. *"But he knows the way that I take; when he has tested me, I will come forth as gold"* (Job 23:10). What a statement of hope! In the midst of his tears, Job understood that God can use suffering as a refiner uses fire to purify gold. During times of fiery trials, all the impurities and dross in our lives melt away.

You can't cope with troubles in this life until you're ready for the next life

Death is evitable, so we need to prepare for it. Until you're ready to die, you're not really ready to live. I've read about a tombstone in a cemetery in England with these words inscribed on it:

> Consider, young man, as you pass by
> As you are now, so once was I.
> As I am now, you soon will be.
> So, prepare, young man, to follow me.

Those are sobering words, but I heard that someone added a note to the tombstone that said:

> To follow you is not my intent
> Until I know which way you went!

Job believed that he would see His Creator after he died. Therefore, he wasn't afraid to think about or talk about it. He confessed that he was looking forward to being renewed and seeing his Creator face to face. We need to remember that we aren't in the land the of the living going to the land of the dying; right now we're in the land of the dying, and we're going to the land of the living. If you have a personal relationship with your Creator, you don't have to fear death.

Hope to Carry on in Tough Times

Job shows us that it is possible to have hope even in the midst of pain. It is this hope for the future that provides us with the strength to carry on today and not quit. It's not hope in hope that works; it's coming to a place where you say, "Though he slay me, yet will I hope in Him!" Have you come to grips with what's going to happen when you die?

Back in the days when doctors used to make house calls, there was as small town physician who walked to his patients' homes, his faithful collie Jake walking by his side. The faithful dog would always wait patiently outside the house while his master finished.

One day the doctor was visiting a man named Luke who was suffering from a terminal illness. As the doctor put away his stethoscope back into his bag, Luke said, "Doc, I'm scared. What can you tell me about death? What's on the other side?" The doctor sighed, sat on the edge of Luke's bed and said, "Luke, I can't tell you much about that..." Then the doctor had a thought. "But I can show you something that might help you."

The doctor got up, opened the door, and called for Jake. The dog suddenly bounded inside the room, gratefully leaping all over his master. The doctor continued, "Luke, my dog has never been in here before. He had no idea what was on the other side of this door. All he knew was that his master was there on the other side. I can't tell you much about what's on the 'other side' of death. But I know you're a Christian, so I can assure you that your Master is waiting there. When he calls, just think of it as running into His arms." Luke smiled, reached out a hand to pat Jake on the head and said, "That's good enough for me."

It was good enough for Job to know that His Creator would *"call and I will answer"* (Job 14:16). You can find that same kind of hope, despite your pain, in Christ. Rest assured that one day He will call you home, and you will answer Him. That's why it's possible for you to face the rest of this life with a HOPEful attitude: Having Only Positive Expectations.

A Life Worth Living

Job's tale is the most famous riches to rags to riches story in all of literature. In the middle of his suffering, Job utters many amazing observations about God and reveals a powerful persistence to trust God throughout his pain. In the next part of Job's story, we get a glimpse of how bad things had become, but at the same time we hear Job express his undying hope and trust in one thing and one thing only. The one thing worth knowing.

"In the depth of winter, I finally learned that there was within me an invincible summer."
—Albert Camus

CHAPTER 9

The One Thing Worth Knowing

In 1991, there was a popular movie named *City Slickers* starring Billy Crystal who played Mitch, a hard driving urban executive whose job and marriage are falling apart. To distract himself from his pain, he convinces some of his city friends to take a trip to a working ranch in New Mexico to learn how to herd cattle.

Jack Palance won an Oscar for his role as the crusty old cowboy named Curley. In one scene, Mitch and Curley are riding alone when Mitch pours out his heart about how miserable his life is. Curley says, "Do you know what the secret to life is?" He holds up his index finger and continues, "This. One thing. Just one thing. You stick with that, and everything else don't mean nuthin'." Mitch replies, "That's great, but what's the one thing? Curly just smiles mysteriously and says, "That's what you gotta' figure out."

Our friend Job had come to that same understanding in the midst of his agony and suffering. What was still worth living for? Job 19:17–20 describes his lowest point:

> *"My breath is offensive to my wife; I am loathsome to my own brothers. Even the little boys scorn me; when I appear, they ridicule me. All my intimate friends detest me; those I love have turned against me. I am nothing but skin and bones; I have escaped with only the*

skin of my teeth."

However, he hung onto the one thing he knew. Job 19:23–27 says: *"Oh, that my words were recorded, that they were written on a scroll, that they were inscribed with an iron tool on lead, or engraved in rock forever! I know that my Redeemer lives, and that in the end he will stand upon the earth. And after my skin has been destroyed, yet in my flesh I will see God; I myself will see him with my own eyes—I, and not another. How my heart yearns within me!"*

Our Relationship with God

What one thing will sustain you through pain? It's knowing Christ as your Redeemer. Job believed that Someone in his future would redeem his life from destruction. He didn't know His name was Jesus. However, we know that Jesus is the Redeemer that Job saw by faith. Job found a unique relationship with God that gave him the peace he needed in the midst of pain.

A Positive Relationship

There were a lot of things Job didn't know. He didn't know why he was suffering. He didn't know why his friends were accusing him. In the midst of his uncertainty, he proclaimed that there was one thing he did know: his Redeemer was real. He didn't say, "I hope," or "I think," or "Perhaps" my Redeemer lives. He was positive. He said, "I KNOW!" In the Hebrew language, the first personal pronoun is intensified. It's like Job said, *"I* know" as opposed to anyone else knowing the answer.

The word "know" means to know by experience. It was a word that carried the concept of intimate knowledge. In Genesis 4, the Bible says that Adam "knew" his wife, Eve—meaning sexual intimacy. Knowing God doesn't come from reading a book or hearing a message. It happens when you meet Jesus

Christ and you begin to know Him in a personal way. Job knew God by experience. He didn't just take a course called *Experiencing God*—he really was experiencing God! Can you say that? Do you have that same assurance to say, "I know, that I know, that I know, that my Redeemer lives?"

An Intimate Relationship

Remember what we learned in an earlier chapter: Job didn't say "I know a Redeemer" or "I know the Redeemer." He said, *"I know that MY Redeemer lives."* The word "my" may denote selfish ownership. It's like when someone says, "That's my car! Get your hands off of it." However, the word "my" can also denote personal connection. For example, when I say, "This is my hand"—I'm expressing my hand's relationship to the rest of my body. When you simply acknowledge that Jesus is ruler over the universe, there's no personal connection. However, when you say Jesus is MY Lord, you're confessing that He is ruler over your life.

Imagine a group of young ladies cooing over a basinet with a new born baby. One says, "She is such a precious baby!" Another says, "What an adorable baby!" A third says, "What a well-behaved baby!" Finally, one of the women speaks up and says, "Thank you, that's *my* baby!" That little word "my" makes a huge difference. One reason so many teenagers and college students go through a time of spiritual crisis is because they have to decide for themselves what they been taught by their parents, pastors, and teachers. Being born in a Christian home doesn't make you a Christian any more than being born in a garage makes you a car. God has no grandchildren. Everyone must come to a place in their lives when they decide to crown Jesus as Lord of their lives.

A Redeeming Relationship

Job didn't say, "I know the Lord lives." He didn't say, "I know God lives." Instead he gave a very precise and specific title for God. He said, *"I know that my REDEEMER lives..."*

Have you ever heard the expression, "It's who you know that matters?" Fred Smith, a well-known Christian leader and member of our congregation, once talked to our staff team about relationships. He said, "It's not who you know that matters; and it's not what you know that matters. It's what you know about who you know that matters!"

That remark earned a good laugh, and as I was chuckling I thought about Job's relationship with our Redeemer. Sure, it's who you know that matters. However, when it comes to knowing God, what do you really know about Him? The best place to find what God is like is in the Bible.

Job used the word "Redeemer" which is *go'el* in Hebrew. In the Old Testament, a *go'el* was someone who "bought back" something valuable that had been lost or forfeited. We see the impact of a redeemer in the biblical story of Ruth. When she and Naomi returned home as widows, they had no claim to any property that Naomi's husband had owned. They were destitute. The hero of the story was the handsome Boaz who fell in love with Ruth and eventually married her. By marrying Ruth, Boaz became the **go'el**, the kinsman redeemer, and was able to reclaim all the property that once belonged to Naomi's family.

This is a wonderful picture of what Jesus, our Redeemer, has done for us. Because of our sinful condition, we have no right to claim the blessings that God originally intended for His creatures. As our **go'el**, Jesus came to pay the price for our sins so that we can be a part of God's family. He is our blessed Redeemer. Titus 2:14 says, *"Jesus Christ gave himself for us to REDEEM us from all wickedness."* He bought us back when He paid the price for our sins on the cross.

I once read a story about a boy who carefully constructed a miniature sailboat. He crafted the wood to fit the planks together and make it watertight. He painted the boat with several layers to make it beautiful. He then cut and sewed a piece of cloth to serve as the sail on the mast. After weeks of hard work, his toy sailboat was ready to sail. He took it to a lake in a city park and shoved it off. Instantly, the sail filled out and the boat quickly sailed across the lake. He ran around the lake as fast as he could to retrieve it, but when he got to the other side he couldn't find it.

The little boy assumed it had sunk and was lost forever. A few days later, he was walking by a toy store and was surprised to see his sailboat displayed in the window. He ran inside and said to the shop owner, "That's my boat!" The owner patiently listened to his story and said, "I'm sorry, son, but a man came in here with this boat a few days ago and I paid him $10 for it. If you want it, I'll sell it to you for $10."

The boy didn't have the money. However, with determination he said, "Sir, I'll get the money. Please don't sell the boat just yet." Over the next few days, the little boy worked to earn the cash. He found extra jobs around his neighborhood raking leaves, collecting bottles, and running errands. Finally he had earned $10, and he raced back to the toy store. He laid several crumpled one-dollar bills and a pocketful of change on the counter. The storekeeper counted the change and handed the sailboat to the proud boy. He walked outside, hugged his sailboat to his chest, and said, "You're twice mine—I made you and now I've bought you back!" That's exactly what our Redeemer, Jesus Christ, has done for us. He made us and then He bought us back from the penalty of sin!

A Living Relationship

I find that it's interesting that even though Job spoke these words almost 4000 years ago, he used the correct tense for the verb "to live." He said, *"I know that my Redeemer lives ... "* He didn't say, "I know my Redeemer LIVED" or "I know that my Redeemer WILL LIVE." The Hebrew verb is *"hay,"* which literally means "living." It's the same word used to describe "the Living God." Job knew that one day he would die, but His Redeemer lives and would live forever.

What makes our faith different than any other religion is that it is a living faith in a living God. Jesus isn't just one of

97

several religious leaders who lived and died. He lived, and He died, but He rose from the dead and is alive forevermore. Do you have a living relationship with Jesus? Perhaps you can recite all the facts about Jesus' life, but that's not the same thing as knowing Him. You can believe that He was born of a virgin, lived a sinless life, died on the cross, and even rose from the dead. Sadly, it's possible to believe all those historical facts about Jesus without actually having a living relationship with Him.

To put it another way, you may believe in Jesus Christ the same way you believe in George Washington. You can affirm that Washington lived and fought for America and was our first President, but you certainly don't know him. In the same way, there is literally an eternity of difference between knowing about Jesus and knowing Jesus. People often ask me if it's possible for them to know for certain they have a living relationship with Jesus. And I usually respond, "Well, have you talked to Him today?" I can't recall ever addressing any words to George Washington throughout my day, but I talk to Jesus several times each day. Why? Because our relationship is a living one.

A Relationship with a Future

Job's affirmation of faith was also a prophetic statement. He said, *"In the end he will stand upon the earth..."* The word "end" means "end of time." Throughout the Bible, we read that one day when Jesus returns He will stand in victory upon the earth. Zechariah describes this final battle with these words, *"Then the Lord will go out and fight against those nations, as he fights in the day of battle. On that day his feet will stand on the Mount of Olives, east of Jerusalem, and the Mount of Olives will be split in two from east to west, with half of the mountain moving north and half moving south"* (Zechariah 14:3–4).

If you are a child of God, you can look forward with eager anticipation to the return of the Lord Jesus. One day our Redeemer will indeed stand upon the earth just as Job said. The

Apostle Paul wrote in 2 Timothy 4:8 that there is a crown of righteousness laid up for *"all those who love his appearing."* Do you long for His appearing? There's a difference between loving Jesus and loving His appearing.

When I was about six or seven, my best buddy Forest and I noticed that the door was open to our neighbor's house, so we went inside and started stealing everything we could carry. As a child, I definitely proved the doctrine of total depravity! We didn't know where we were going to hide the loot—we hadn't thought that far ahead yet. As we were leaving the house, loaded down with everything we could carry, the neighbor drove up and caught us red-handed. She grabbed me by the ear and marched over to our house and told my mother what I had done. My mother was so mad she could hardly speak. She did something that, as far as I can remember, she only did once during my childhood. She called my dad at work and told him to come home and punish me. I can remember sitting out on the steps just waiting for my dad to drive up. I loved my dad, but I sure didn't love his appearing that day!

Is that the way you feel about the return of Christ? You love Him, but you're not too excited about the prospect of Him arriving anytime soon? If so, why don't you examine your heart and see if there are some attitudes and actions that you could confess and quit in order to be ready for His return? We should all live in such an expectant state that we can say like the Apostle John on the last page of the Bible, "Even so, Lord Jesus, come quickly!"

A Permanent Relationship

Job knew that he was going to die, yet he confessed that death wouldn't be the end of his existence. This is what he meant when he said, *"In my flesh, I will SEE GOD ..."* We live in a throwaway world where we can count on little being permanent. In fact, death will alter every human relationship, no matter how permanent they may seem on earth. The one relationship that death won't change is our relationship with Jesus; it's our only permanent relationship. For that reason, Job didn't fear death, and neither should we.

William Randolph Hearst (1863-1951) was one of the wealthiest and most powerful men of the 20th Century. At the peak of his media career, he was worth over $500,000,000. He built an enormous castle in the hills near San Simeon in California. It had 90,000 square feet and took 28 years to build. It is one of the largest, most opulent homes in America, rivaling the Biltmore Estate in North Carolina. Hearst often invited the Hollywood elite to visit with him in his castle. It was a mark of a celebrity's true star status if they were invited to Hearst's castle for a weekend. When the guests arrived, the staff informed them of one very strict rule. In fact, if they broke this rule, they would be immediately escorted off the property and never invited to return. The rule was that whenever the guests were in Hearst's presence, they could never utter the word, "death." Hearst possessed a horrible fear of death. He was so afraid that when one of the palm trees at San Simeon died unexpectedly, the gardeners painted its leaves green until it could be replaced at a time when Hearst was gone. This wealthy tycoon did everything he could to ignore and delay death, but even with his great wealth and power, he couldn't prevent it from happening. On August 14, 1951 he died, and as the Bible says, Hearst faced judgment.

Do you realize that everything we can see around us is temporary? All the mansions, all the skyscrapers, all the money, all the fame will one day disappear. However, to know Jesus is to be a part of something permanent. The Bible says in 2 Corinthians 4:18: *"So we fix our eyes not on what is seen but what is unseen. For what is seen is temporary, but what is unseen is eternal."* While Job was suffering in this world, there was another world that he couldn't see with his physical eyes. However, he believed that one day he would see his Redeemer face to face.

An Exciting Relationship

As Job looked forward to the time when he would see his Redeemer face to face he said, *"How my heart yearns within me!"* Whenever he thought about it, his heart would beat a little faster, a smile would creep onto his face, and a tear would fill his eye. He was passionate about seeing His Redeemer. Knowing God isn't a boring, bland, complacent experience. The fact that we can personally know the God of the Universe is the most exciting truth you'll ever discover!

Is there anything in this life or the next life that you're passionate about? Is there anything that makes your heart beat faster whenever you think about it? Are you truly excited about your faith? If you aren't, you may be substituting a boring religion for a thrilling relationship.

In Philippians 3, the Apostle Paul recounted all the advantages and educational accomplishments that he had enjoyed from birth. Then he wrote that all of his physical, intellectual, and educational pedigrees were nothing compared with knowing Jesus. He was passionate when he wrote: *"What is more, I consider everything a loss compared to the surpassing greatness of knowing Christ Jesus my Lord, for whose sake I have lost all things. I consider them rubbish that I may gain Christ...I want to know Christ and the power of his resurrection and the fellowship of sharing in his sufferings, becoming like him in his death"* (Philippians 3:8, 10).

Life's Most Valuable Discovery

In 1940, a Canadian geologist by the name of John Williamson was working in the African country of Tanzania. One rainy day, his truck got stuck up to its axles in the mud. Pulling out his shovel, Williamson started digging into the mud to free his truck. After a few minutes, his shovel struck something solid. He reached down into the muck and brought out a large, pink-colored stone. As a geologist, he soon realized that he had uncovered a huge diamond—54 karats. That diamond, called the Williamson Pink, is in London among the other Crown

101

Jewels belonging to Queen Elizabeth. It is worth millions of dollars, but it is not for sale at any price.

You might think that if you made that one discovery, it would change your life. There is actually one discovery more life-changing than finding a fortune in the mud. In Matthew 13:44 Jesus said, *"The Kingdom of heaven is like treasure hidden in a field. When a man found it, he hid it again, and then in his joy went and sold all he had and bought that field."* The hidden treasure is the one thing worth knowing: Jesus Christ. When you discover what it means to know Jesus as your Savior and Lord, every other religious notion you've heard will pale in comparison. Instead, you'll give your relationship with Christ everything you have. When Job discovered that knowing his Redeemer was the one thing worth knowing, he found what he was looking for—and he found it in the most unusual place. He found peace—right in the middle of his pain.

A Stranger Enters the Picture
Most of the book of Job is devoted to a cycle of conversations that Job had with Zophar, Bildad, and Eliphaz. However, in Job 32, we discover another character that had been standing by listening to their conversations. Who was he? Another so-called friend? An angel or demon? Whoever he was, we'll discover in the next chapter that he had quite an impact on Job with what he had to say.

"Wisdom is nothing more than healed pain."

–Robert Gary Lee

CHAPTER 10

The
Wisdom of Youth

~~◈~~

Elihu enters the conversation with Job late in the story. He was younger than the other three friends, but besides the age difference there's another important distinction about young Elihu. In Job 33:1–4 he says, *"I am about to open my mouth; my words are on the tip of my tongue. My words come from an upright heart; my lips sincerely speak what I know. The Spirit of God has made me; the breath of the Almighty gives me life."* The Hebrew word for "breath" is *ruach*—it is the same word for "spirit." Zophar, Bildad, and Eliphaz all freely expressed their personal opinions about why Job was suffering, while Elihu spoke under the leadership of the breath of God: the Spirit.

Let's read about this young man on the sidelines in Job 32:1–10:

> *So these three men stopped answering Job, because he was righteous in his own eyes. But Elihu son of Barakel the Buzite, of the family of Ram, became very angry with Job for justifying himself rather than God. He was also angry with the three friends, because they had found no way to refute Job, and yet had condemned him. Now Elihu had waited before speaking to Job because they were older than he. But when he saw that the three men had*

nothing more to say, his anger was aroused.

So, Elihu son of Barakel the Buzite said: "I am young in years and you are old; that is why I was fearful, not daring to tell you what I know. I thought, 'Age should speak; advanced years should teach wisdom.' But it is the spirit in a man, the breath of the Almighty, that gives him understanding. It is not only the old who are wise, not only the aged who understand what is right. Therefore I say: Listen to me; I too will tell you what I know...

Youth is a relative term, but Elihu might have been in his 20s or 30s. We often equate age with wisdom, but there's more wisdom in a Spirit-filled young person than in an older person who merely expresses his or her own opinions. That's because age and experience don't always create wisdom. For instance, there were two employees in a certain business who had both applied for the same promotion. One employee had worked for the company three years, and the other had been there fifteen years. When the younger worker got the promotion, the older employee complained to the boss, "How could you give the promotion to him? I've got fifteen years of experience and he only has three." The boss said, "You don't really have fifteen years experience. You've got one year's experience fifteen times."

Hopefully, as we grow older, we grow wiser, but that doesn't always happen. Wisdom comes from God—age only seasons it. Because he was speaking by the Spirit of God, Elihu expressed more wisdom than the other three friends combined. He made three amazing and accurate observations about God.

God Is More Gracious Than We Deserve
The arguments of Zophar, Bildad, and Eliphaz expressed the belief that people basically get what they deserve. To them, God was an unflinching judge who meted out His punishment

during this lifetime. Good people deserve good treatment, and bad people deserve bad treatment. Their reasoning was that since Job was suffering, Job must have been a wicked man. Elihu countered their argument by saying that God is gracious. Beginning in Job 33:22, Elihu shares the plan of salvation, beginning with our depravity. He says of humanity, *"His soul draws near to the pit, and his life to the messengers of death."* Like all people, we are sinners who deserve death and hell. All of us draw near to the pit, or hell. Elihu mentioned the pit four times in these few verses.

He continues in Job 33:23–25, *"Yet if there is an angel* (messenger) *on his side as a mediator, one out of a thousand, to tell a man what is right for him, to be gracious to him and say, 'Spare him from going down to the pit; I have found a ransom for him'—then his flesh is renewed like a child's; it is restored as in the days of his youth."* This reference to an angel could mean a human messenger. The Hebrew word for angel is *malach,* which also means "messenger." I believe that Elihu was the messenger that God sent to share His truth with Job and with us. God's message to lost humanity is that He has paid the ransom for sinners so we don't have to go down into the pit of destruction. When we accept the benefits of the atoning death of Jesus Christ, it's like being born again! Or, as Elihu expressed it, it's like being restored to the days of youth.

Next, Elihu tells us what we must do once we have heard God's message of grace. In Job 33:26 he says, *"He prays to God and finds favor with him, he sees God's face and shouts for joy; he is restored by God to his righteous state."* First, you must learn that you are a sinner and deserve death and hell. However, through God's grace, He has provided His Son to pay the ransom for your sins. Your response is to simply seek God and accept His forgiveness. Once you receive His forgiveness by grace, He will replace your guilt with incredible joy.

To see the next phase of personal salvation—a public profession of faith—read Job 33:27–30: *"Then he comes to men and says, 'I sinned and perverted what was right, but I did not get what I deserved* (that's what grace is). *He redeemed my soul from going down to the pit, and I will live to enjoy light. God does all these things to a man—twice even three times—to turn back his soul from the pit, that the light of life may shine on him."*

Did you follow that progression? First, you hear the message of grace, and then you respond by receiving God's free gift of grace. Then you will want to tell others about God's grace. Your testimony will be, "I sinned, but praise God—I didn't get what I deserved!" However, I've heard people sometimes complain because they don't think they are getting what they deserve. You'll never hear me say that! I believe that I deserve death and hell and an eternity separated from God in the pit of destruction because of my sin. I don't want what I deserve; I want what I *need*: grace and mercy. In fact, the very definition of grace is God giving me what I need rather than what I deserve. That's why salvation is a gift that you can't earn or buy. The Bible says, *"For it is by grace you have been saved, through faith—and this not from yourselves, it is the gift of God"* (Ephesians 2: 8).

Let's imagine that you invite me into your home for a delicious meal, along with some wonderful conversation and fellowship. When it's time to leave, I reach in my pocket, pull out a dime, and place it in your hand. "I enjoyed the meal," I say, "but I'm sure it cost you a lot of money, so I want to pay you this dime for the food I ate." What an insult! Of course, I would never do that because I would insult your gracious hospitality. Nevertheless, when God offers us the free gift of salvation by grace, some people still "pull out a dime" and try to pay their way to heaven. Elihu was right on target. God is more gracious than we deserve.

Songs in the Night

There are some precious nuggets of gold that often lie hidden within the pages of your Bible. One of them is Elihu's great insight into human behavior in Job 35:9–10: *"Men cry out under a load of oppression; they plead for relief from the arm of the powerful. But no one says, 'Where is God my Maker, who gives songs in the night?'"* Can you relate to that? Are you suffering under a load of oppression like Job? The natural reaction when we suffer is to cry out for relief. We want God to remove the unpleasant circumstances, but Elihu says that in the midst of our deepest pain, we should look for God. He is the One who gives us songs to sing despite the darkness.

To find peace in your pain, just meditate on that thought for a few moments. Notice the setting of this scripture: during the night. Nighttime is when our fears and worries often grow out of proportion. We all fear those things that go "bump in the night"—those clumsy worries that rattle around in our minds when we're trying to sleep. Those who struggle with depression understand the meaning of going through "the dark night of the soul." In addition to the setting, think about the song. A song speaks of joy and peace. The good news is that whenever you struggle within the darkest time in your life, God can give you a song to lighten your heart. It may be a praise chorus or line from a hymn that comes to mind.

I have an eclectic taste in music and enjoy a wide variety of genres. God is the Creator of all music, but some people have stolen it to communicate a false message. For instance, I enjoy listening to music by Enya, even though she's the queen of New Age music. A few years ago, I was listening to a song she recorded called, "How Can I Keep from Singing?" It contained the phrase from Job about "songs in the night," so I suspected it was an old hymn. I did some research and discovered that it was, in fact, a hymn written by Robert Lowery in 1860.

I also discovered that Enya's version altered the most important words of the hymn, presumably to fit her New Age belief. She sings about hearing the "truth" that "liveth." However, the original words of the hymn are about hearing the Lord, "my Savior," who liveth! Truth doesn't give you songs in the night—God does. Once you understand that, you can't keep from singing—even in the darkest nights of your life.

It's easy to sing when everything is going great. However, God promises to give us a song when our circumstances are difficult. A great example of this is in the Book of Acts. While they were in Philippi, Paul and Silas had been arrested and severely beaten. Then they were thrown into the deepest part of the dungeon with their feet constrained in stocks—bleeding and facing possible execution. According to Acts 16:25–26: *"About midnight Paul and Silas were praying and singing hymns to God, and the other prisoners were listening to them. Suddenly there was such a violent earthquake that the foundations of the prison were shaken. At once, all the prison doors flew open, and everybody's chains came loose."*

God gave these two prisoners songs in the night, just as Elihu said. There is a twofold blessing to the songs that God gives in the night. First, these songs give a sense of peace and joy. Second, when you sing praise to God in the night, you'll discover that you are set free from the fear and worries that bind you. God really does give us songs in the night. Are you listening? Better yet, are you joining in with the song that He puts in your heart?

God Is Greater Than We Can Comprehend

The last thing that Elihu teaches us about God is that we don't have the mental competence to understand the works and ways of the Almighty God. He says in Job: 37:14–18, *"Listen to this Job; stop and consider God's wonders. Do you know how God controls the clouds and makes his lightning flash? Do you know how the clouds hang poised, those wonders of him who is perfect in knowledge? You who swelter in your clothes when the land lies hushed under the south wind, can you join him in spreading out the skies hard as a mirror of cast bronze?"* Not only does God reign beyond our galaxy, He is also beyond our ability to understand. We tend to think we're pretty smart, but Elihu reminds us that while we're down here sweating, God is painting His next original sunset.

Then Elihu says in Job 37:19, *"Tell us what we should say*

to him; we cannot draw up our case because of our darkness."
If we compared intellect with brightness, God would be the
sun, and we would be the dimmest bulb in the socket. You can
try looking directly into the sun, but you'll injure your eyes
doing it. In the same way, you can try to stand on the same
intellectual level as God, but you'll find it impossible. Elihu
continues in Job 37: 21–24, *"Now no one can look at the sun,
bright as it is in the skies after the wind has swept them clean.
Out of the north he comes in golden splendor; God comes
in awesome majesty. The Almighty is beyond our reach and
exalted in power; in his justice and great righteousness he does
not oppress. Therefore, men revere him, for does he not have
regard for all the wise in heart?"*

Elihu sounded like a spiritual meteorologist as he
appealed to Job to consider the amazing mystery of weather.
Today, we have radar and satellite images to forecast and
track the weather, but we basically haven't advanced any from
Job's day. Everybody talks about the weather, but nobody ever
does anything about it! Even today, only God can control the
weather. Jesus says that He makes the rain to fall on the just
and the unjust.

I remember hearing a humorous story about a preacher
in Kansas who arrived back in town after a tornado nearly
leveled the town. At the train station, he ran into a dishonest
businessman with a reputation for cheating. The man was
distraught because his house had been blown away by the
tornado. The preacher smugly said to the man, "That should
teach you that God always punishes sin." The man then said
to the preacher, "Oh really? And did you know that your house
was also blown away by the storm?" The preacher paused and
said with a gulp, "That teaches us that the Lord's ways are
beyond our understanding."

Perhaps Elihu used the weather as an illustration of God's
greatness because he could see a storm brewing on the horizon
as they spoke. Soon, the storm struck and another Speaker
interrupted him. Job 38:1 says, *"Then the Lord answered Job*

out of the storm ..." And with that phrase, God brings us to the climax of the story. Up to that point, Job had been asking God a multitude of questions, yet heaven was silent. Finally, God spoke, but He didn't deliver a set of clean, concise answers. Instead, God starts asking Job a few questions of His own. God basically said to Job, "I'll answer your questions when you answer mine."

Then God proceeded to ask Job 65 questions—none of which Job could answer correctly.

Are you struggling with questions today? Maybe you've lost your job and you're asking, "Why?" Perhaps you are struggling with cancer or some debilitating pain and you're wanting to know, "Why, Lord?" Like Job, you can ask your questions. Just don't expect to receive nice, clear, concise answers. His greatness is beyond our comprehension. His ways are not our ways and His thoughts are not our thoughts.

If I Had Been in Charge of Creation...
If God had delegated Creation to me, I would have done things differently. I would have created a world where there is no disease or accidents, no killer hurricanes, no terrorism, and no babies born with congenital defects. And, by the way, no spiders or mosquitoes!

God created a world just like that in the Garden. However, he also created something extremely powerful—human choice. He didn't create us as zombies or robots who automatically bow before Him and love Him. When humanity chose to sin, we unleashed a horrible chain reaction of natural and accidental evil in the world.

Likewise, Job possessed the ability to choose to love God—even in the midst of His pain. If Job only loved God when things were going well in His life, his love would not have been authentic. Job would have proved Satan right. However, Job faced more suffering than any of us will ever endure, and still he chose to love God.

God didn't cause these evils to come upon Job any more

than He has caused you to suffer. God doesn't inflict evil. However, during the most painful episodes of our lives, God can speak to us through the pain unlike any other time. C.S. Lewis (who lost his wife to cancer) wrote, "We can rest contentedly in our sins and in our stupidities, and anyone who has watched gluttons shoveling down the most exquisite foods as if they did not know what they were eating, will admit that we can ignore even pleasure. However, pain insists that we attend to it. God whispers to us in our pleasures, speaks in our consciences, but shouts in our pains. It is his megaphone to rouse a deaf world."[15]

What was God shouting to Job? "Don't lose hope in Me." In response, Job said, "Though he slay me, yet will I hope in him!" When the pain increased, God's voice became even stronger, "Job, even with your unanswered questions, trust Me!" By faith, Job said, "I know that my Redeemer lives, and in the end I will see Him." God is saying, even shouting, the same thing to you amid the noise and confusion of your pain. But how do you hear and recognize His voice? That's what this next chapter is all about.

"What man actually needs is not a tensionless state but rather the striving and struggling for some goal worthy of him. What he needs is not the discharge of tension at any cost, but the call of a potential meaning waiting to be fulfilled by him."

—Victor Frankl

CHAPTER 11

Hearing God's Voice in the Storm

I've always been fascinated with the history of U.S. Presidents. One of my favorite Presidents was Calvin Coolidge. He was a man of few words, but the words he spoke were often blunt. Knowing his reputation for cryptic answers, a journalist once said, "Mr. President I made a $100 bet with another journalist that I could get you to say more than three words. Would you care to comment?" Calvin Coolidge smiled and said, "You lose." That's how he got the nickname "Silent Cal."

Some people consider our Creator to be a "Silent God." When they are going through painful trials and tribulations, they cry out to God, asking why. As they pause to listen for a reply, it seems as if heaven is silent. However, the Bible teaches that God has spoken and still speaks today—we just may not be listening carefully enough. Sometimes God even allows a storm to spin into our lives so that we will listen more intently.

Job often ping-ponged between faith and doubt. His faith bent, but it did not break. As Job defended himself against the accusations of others, he asked God to answer him. However, for most of the book, God's silence brews like a thunderstorm, quietly building strength. Finally, the storm breaks in all its fury and that's when God chooses to speak: out of the storm.

In the opening refrains of his thunderous message to Job, God said, *"Who is this that darkens my counsel with words without knowledge? Brace yourself like a man; I will question you, and you shall answer me"* (Job 38:1–3). The Bible tells us God answered Job "out of the storm" (v1). Now when it says that God "answered" Job, that doesn't mean that God gave Job the answers he was seeking. Instead of giving Job an answer, God actually started asking Job questions! By the time He finishes, God will ask Job over 180 questions. Let's take a look at just a few.

GOD ASKS: Where were you when I created the earth?

In Job 38:4–7, God asks, *"Where were you when I laid the earth's foundation? Tell me, if you understand. Who marked off its dimensions? Surely you know! Who stretched a measuring line across it? On what were its footings set, or who laid its cornerstone—while the morning stars sang together and the angels shouted for joy?"* The point of this chapter isn't to address the ongoing debate between whether we came into existence by Divine creation or whether we are the product of blind chance and random evolution. I never apologize for believing that God created the heavens and the earth, and I think we should teach Intelligent Design and Creation alongside the theory of evolution. Nevertheless, the Bible is not a science textbook that tells us *how* we were created. It is God's love letter that tells us *why* we were created. Humanity is arrogant enough to suggest how life began, but every explanation science offers is pure speculation and hypothesis because, as God reminded Job, nobody was around to observe creation.

GOD ASKS: How many sunrises have you made?

The Bible teaches that God not only created the universe, but that He also maintains it. Planet earth is orbiting around the sun at a speed of 66,000 mph, while at the same time it is spinning on a fixed axis at about 1,000 mph. Because of this rotation, one half of the globe is facing the sun while the other is in darkness. If this didn't occur every day, one side of the planet would freeze, and the other side would burn up. Every morning, the sun rises in a different place because the planet also gradually

116

tilts on its axis 23 degrees to create the different seasons. Otherwise, each hemisphere would be too cold or too hot to support life. This is a meticulous operation—and it boggles the imagination to think that this all happens by pure accident. This is why God says to Job in chapter 38:12–13, *"Have you ever given orders to the morning, or shown the dawn its place, that it might take the earth by the edges and shake the wicked out of it?"* Every sunrise has God's signature on it. It is His reminder to appreciate another day as His gift to us. Until we can control the orbit, spinning, and tilting of the planet, we'd better keep quiet about how smart we think we are.

GOD ASKS: Are you older than light?
In Job 38:19–21, God asked Job tongue-in-cheek, *"What is the way to the abode of light? And where does darkness reside? Can you take them to their places? Do you know the paths to their dwellings? Surely you know, for you were already born! You have lived so many years!"* I like this question because it proves that God has a sense of humor. Hebrew humor often pictured the absurd—like when Jesus talks about screening out a gnat and swallowing a camel. God gently poked fun at Job by sarcastically suggesting that if Job was so smart, he must have been around a long time—before light even existed. Albert Einstein contended that the only constant in the physical universe is light. He used it as the key factor to demonstrate the relationship between mass and energy ($E=mc^2$). Today, scientists measure light and use light, but they still don't understand what light really is. Yet the Bible simply says in 1 John 1:5, *"God is light,"* which means that He is older and wiser than any living being.

GOD ASKS: Can you control the stars?
From ancient times, people have gazed up into the star-filled sky at night and tried to find some kind of order or meaning. Those who ascribe to astrology say that the position of the stars and planets controls our lives. However, I'd rather trust the

One who made the stars and controls the constellations. God asks, *"Can you bind the beautiful Pleiades? Can you loose the cords of Orion? Can you bring forth the constellations in their seasons or lead out the Bear with its cubs? Do you know the laws of the heavens?"* (Job 38:31–32).

About 7,000 stars can be seen by the naked eye. By connecting the dots, ancient people saw the shapes of various people and animals. For instance, Orion is the figure of the mighty hunter who moved across the sky in the winter. They noticed that the stars seemed to wheel around the sky, but there was one star, the North Star, that served as the pivot point for this rotation. Ancient mariners were able to use the North Star (and the Southern Cross in the Southern hemisphere) to guide them.

We're still gazing at the stars today; we're just using powerful telescopes to aid our vision. With the cheapest consumer telescope, you can see a million stars. However, even using the Hubble telescope, astronomers still have no clue about how many stars there are. They estimate that there are over a billion stars in our galaxy, the Milky Way. And the Milky Way is only one of millions of galaxies! The deeper we peer into space, the more mysteries we find. We'd like to believe we're in control of our lives, but we can't even *begin* to take control of the stars. As the Psalmist declared three thousand years ago, *"When I consider the heavens, the work of your fingers, the moon and the stars which you have set in place, what is man that you are mindful of him?"* (Psalm 8:3–4).

GOD ASKS: Do all the animals depend on you?

I imagine Job sitting there, stone-faced, as the questions just keep on coming. *"Do you know when the mountain goats give birth? Do you watch when the doe bears her fawn? Do you count the months till they bear? Do you know the time they give birth?... Does the hawk take flight by your wisdom and spread his wings toward the south? Does the eagle soar at your command and build his nest on high?"* (39:1–2, 26–27). If you love animals, you should read all of Job 39 because you'll find you have something in common with your Father. Did you know He takes the time to preside at the birth of every little fawn? Jesus said that God notices whenever a tiny sparrow falls to the earth (Matthew 10:19). God is such a powerful, caring Creator that He presides at the birth and death of all of the animals.

This chapter could be subtitled "God's Animal Planet" because He takes credit for creating and designing all the different species in the animal kingdom. Have you ever wondered how many animal species there are? About a million different species have been identified (750,000 are insects), but the Smithsonian Institute estimates that there are 30 million different species on the planet! Humanity arrogantly thinks that they are self-reliant, at the top of the food chain, but even the animals are wise enough to look entirely to God for their needs.

GOD ASKS: Do you think you can correct me?

Up to that point, Job had been demanding that God answer him. However, now we see that the Creator deflects that same logic back onto Job. He basically says, "When you answer me, Job, I'll be glad to answer you!" With that, the Lord continues His quiz.

"The Lord said to Job: 'Will the one who contends with the Almighty correct him? Let him who accuses God answer him!'...Then Job answered the Lord: 'I am unworthy—how can I reply to you? I put my hand over my mouth. I spoke once, but I have no answer—twice, but I will say no more.'" (40:1–2, 3–5). Job was finally ready to slap his hand over his mouth, shut up, and just listen. When we're going through seasons of sufferings, we tend to ask God all kinds of questions. God doesn't owe us any answers, but He can still comfort us and give us peace beyond understanding.

119

God Still Speaks to Us in Our Storms

God speaks to His children in many different ways. He spoke to Moses through a burning bush. He used a whale to get Jonah's attention. He used a donkey to speak to Balaam, and He even used a rooster to speak to Simon Peter. He spoke to Job out of a whirlwind. According to *Strong's Exhaustive Concordance*, the word *whirlwind* can be translated "hurricane." God still speaks to His children during storms. Personal storms come in many shapes and sizes: financial hurricanes, relational whirlwinds and emotional or physical thundershowers. Whenever you find yourself in the eye of a personal storm, it's a perfect time to listen for God's voice.

Why does God speak to us in our storms? I think it's because some of us are so hard-headed that we aren't really paying attention when our emotional climate is sunny and mild. However, when the hurricane warnings sound, we tend to stop and pay attention.

An old sailor once said that during the fiercest storms, the only thing way a ship can survive is for the helmsman to keep her nose pointed straight into the wind. If he tries to turn to the left or the right, the ship may capsize. If he tries to run from the wind, the waves can surge over the stern. That's good advice for life. Whenever you're in a storm, don't turn away from God. Don't run *from* Him. Instead, boldly turn straight toward Him and seek His face. When you're in the sunshine, you *may* have faith, but when you're in the storm you *must* have faith to survive.

I Am Speechless before God's Power and Wisdom

Earlier, Job had confidently boasted that if he could face God that he would strut right over and cross examine Him. In Job 23:3–4 he said, *"Oh, that I knew where I might find him, that I might come even to his seat! I would lay my case before him and fill my mouth with arguments."* That attitude reminds me of the blow-hard lion in the Wizard of Oz. Before he entered the wizard's courts, he bragged, "Let me at him! I'll show him a thing or two!" Then when he finally faced the wizard, he crouched in trembling fright. Likewise, when God finally showed up in Job's presence, he found himself speechless.

Like Job, have you ever wanted to play Larry King Live with God? Job imagined the Almighty sitting across the desk from him as he peppered Him with questions. "Okay, God, I want to know why I lost my fortune, my family, and my health. I'm going to ask the questions, and you're going to give me some answers." I've heard people look around at the injustices in this world and say, "When I get to heaven, I'm going to have a lot of questions for God!" I used to say it myself. However, I stopped saying it years ago. Why? When we enter the presence of a Holy God, we aren't going to be on a level with Him where we can demand a bunch of answers. One of my favorite songs is "I Can Only Imagine" by Mercy Me. It's a conversation with God about what we'll do when we first see Him in heaven. Will we dance? Sing? I don't know for sure what will happen, but my vote is not for dancing right away. I'm for falling on my face, totally speechless in God's presence.

That's what Job did after God finished speaking. He simply said, "I am unworthy." The King James Version translates that phrase, "I am vile." It's the Hebrew word *qalal* that literally means "lightweight." Compared to the God of the Universe, Job admitted that he was an intellectual featherweight. He was overwhelmed by God's greatness and underwhelmed by his own ignorance. When you truly see God for who He is, you get smaller and smaller and God gets bigger and bigger. Not only that, in the awesome presence of God, you will discover that all your questions and your arguments grow smaller and smaller. Every question God issued to Job announced this underlying powerful truth: "I am God. That means you're not." Until we know a little bit more about running the physical universe, we can't tell God how to run the moral universe.

I Find Peace in My Pain When I Surrender
We often read theologians who write about the "sovereignty

121

of God," but most people have no idea what that really means. The root of the word is "reign." The prefix *sove* means "over." Therefore, sovereignty means to "rule and reign over," which is exactly what God does. Here's my definition of God's sovereignty in seven words: His right to do whatever He pleases.

God didn't owe Job an explanation, and He doesn't owe me one. Even so, God is not some malignant, capricious deity getting a degree of malicious pleasure by keeping people bewildered. No, God is a loving Father who grieves when His children are hurting.

In the discussion about the sovereignty of God, the inevitable question arises: "Do people have a free will to choose? Or is God, in His sovereignty, controlling everything?" The answer is "yes" to both questions! God will not be confined to the logical parameters that we try to impose on Him. How do can you balance free will with the absolute sovereignty of God? Perhaps this crude illustration will help you understand.

As I'm writing this chapter, I happen to be on a Delta Airlines 777 flying from Tel Aviv, Israel to Atlanta. Whenever we fly, we're choosing to place our trust in many people. At this moment, I'm placing my trust in the law of aerodynamics. When the forces of thrust, drag, lift, and gravity are balanced, then flight takes place. I'm also putting my trust in the pilots who are flying this jet. In addition, I'm putting my faith in the engineers and workers at Boeing Corporation who designed and built the jet. Boarding this jet was a choice on my part–an act of faith and free will. However, once I board the plane and the door shuts, the destination has already been determined by Delta. I have no control over whether or not we arrive— it's under the control of others. This is a faint picture of the sovereignty of God. He has already determined the ultimate destination of your life—that's why it's called pre-destination. Of course, as a passenger on this jet, I'm not bound by chains and unable to move. I do have a seat belt I can unfasten when the captain "has determined that it is safe to move about the cabin." Once that light goes off, I'm free. I have choices on the flight as well. I can choose to enjoy some delicious airline food—or I'm free to decline. The flight attendant isn't going to force feed me. I can choose to sleep or to watch a movie. While I'm making these choices, the jet is moving steadily toward the pre-determined location of Atlanta. There is both freedom and sovereignty in play, and they do not contradict each other.

I think this can be applied to God's sovereignty and our freedom to choose. Like the jet I'm traveling in now, God is moving His creation steadily toward the goal that He purposed in Christ before the world began (see Ephesians 1:4–5). Within that Divine design, He has given us the freedom to make moral and spiritual choices. Therefore, Job chose to surrender to God's sovereignty.

When God Shows Up

One of my favorite scenes from the movie Forrest Gump is when Lt. Dan and Forrest are out on his shrimp boat. Lt. Dan lost both his legs in Vietnam, and he was angry and bitter because he hadn't died on the battlefield. Forrest and Lt. Dan weren't catching any shrimp, so Lt. Dan sarcastically told Forrest he ought to go to church and pray that God would give them some shrimp. So Forrest did. On their next trip, they still didn't catch any shrimp. Lt. Dan asks, "Where's this God of yours?" At that moment, a hurricane blows in. Looking back, Forrest says, "It's funny that Lt. Dan would ask that because right then, God showed up."

During the storm, Forrest was scared, but Lt. Dan was angry. At the height of the hurricane, he is swinging at the top of the mast, screaming out to God, "It's time you and me had a showdown! You call this a storm?" However, after the storm passes, Lt. Dan was a changed man. Forrest replies as the narrator, "He never actually said so, but I think [Lt. Dan] made his peace with God."

Have you truly made your peace with God? You may be going through a crisis right now. If you aren't, don't worry, the next one is just around the corner. However, you don't have to be afraid. He is far greater, and far more caring than we can ever understand. God never intended for us to understand Him; He just wants us to trust Him.

You'll never experience His peace until you hear His voice in the storm. You won't likely hear Him answer your questions of "Why?" or "Why me?" However, like Job discovered, once you open your eyes, then you'll shut your mouth. The questions will subside when you look around at the greatness of God. As we'll see in this next chapter, the key is to accept that life just doesn't make perfect sense this side of heaven. Sometimes we run out of answers. But what then? What do we do in those frustrating moments? If you want to experience God's supernatural peace in your life despite the uncertainties, there are specific steps you must take.

"The mind is its own place, and in itself, can make heaven of Hell, and a hell of Heaven."

–John Milton

CHAPTER 12

What to Do When You Run out of Answers

If Job were a contestant on a game show, chapter 40 would be the double jeopardy round. Job didn't do very well in round one; in fact, at this point, he has run out of answers. When you fast forward to Job 42:1–6, you find Job's response to both rounds of God's questions.

> *Then Job replied to the Lord: "I know that you can do all things; no plan of yours can be thwarted." You asked, "Who is this that obscures my counsel without knowledge?" Surely I spoke of things I did not understand, things too wonderful for me to know. You said, "Listen now, and I will speak; I will question you, and you will answer me." My ears had heard of you but now my eyes have seen you. Therefore I despise myself and repent in dust and ashes.*

If Job wanted to continue his argument, he would have said something like, "Yeah, I heard what you said…but it's just not fair that I'm suffering! What are you going to *do* about it?" I suspect that if Job had persisted in his resistance against God, that would have been the sad ending of a tragic tale. We probably wouldn't even be reading about Job! Instead, Job finally responds to God in the proper way. When you're struggling with pain, try doing what Job did.

Acknowledge God's Unlimited Power

When you feel powerless in your circumstances, one of the first things you can do is to acknowledge God's unlimited power. Job did that when he said, *"I know You can do all things; no plan of Yours can be thwarted"* (Job 42:2). He made this great confession after God described two monstrous animals: behemoth and leviathan in Job 40 and 41. God's description of these two creatures is both fascinating and mysterious. The footnotes of the NIV translation say that behemoth is a hippopotamus and that leviathan is a crocodile. The English artist, William Blake, portrayed them as a type of hippopotamus and a dragon. These are just guesses—and I think they are poor ones.

I agree with the Bible scholars who suggest that a behemoth was actually a dinosaur whose scientific name is Brachiosaurus. The Hebrew word, "behemoth," simply means "enormous creature." Notice the way God described a behemoth in Job 40:15–19: *"Look at the behemoth that I made along with you and which feeds on grass like an ox. What strength he has in his loins and power in the muscles of his belly! His tail sways like a cedar* (that rules out a hippo or an elephant!)*; the sinews of his thighs are close-knit. His bones are tubes of bronze, his limbs like rods of iron. He ranks first among the works of God,* (that could mean it was the largest land animal ever created) *yet his maker can approach him with the sword."* (That may be a reference to the fact that the Brachiosaurus is now extinct.) Let's compare this description with a Brachiosaurus, one of the largest land animals ever to walk on earth. Three times as tall as a giraffe, it was almost 80 feet long and weighed up to 88 tons (compare that to the largest African elephant on record at 10 tons).

So, if the behemoth was likely a dinosaur, what was a leviathan? Again, I agree with those who suggest that this is a description of another prehistoric sea creature called Kronosaurus. (Leviathan is also mentioned in Isaiah 27:1 and Psalm 104 as a mighty sea creature.) Scientists believe that

128

Kronosaurus was a sea creature whose head was head nine feet long and filled with razor sharp teeth that were ten inches long. Crocodiles are scary, but we've captured them and put them in zoos. However, a leviathan was so large and fierce that it couldn't be captured.

Here's God's description of leviathan in Job 41:1ff:

> *"Can you pull in the Leviathan with a fishhook, or tie down his tongue with a rope?... Can you fill his hide with harpoons, or his head with fishing spears? If you lay a hand on him, you will remember the struggle and never do it again! Any hope of subduing him is false, the mere sight of him is overpowering. No one is fierce enough to rouse him. Who then is able to stand against me? Who has a claim against me that I must pay? Everything under heaven belongs to me. I will not fail to speak of his limbs, his strength and his graceful form. Who can strip off his outer coat? Who would approach him with a bridle? Who dares open the doors of his mouth, ringed about with his fearsome teeth? His back has rows of shields tightly sealed together; each one is so close to the next that no air can pass between...He makes the depths churn like a boiling caldron and stirs up the sea like a pot of ointment. Behind him he leaves a glistening wake; one would think the deep had white hair. Nothing on earth is its equal—a creature without fear."*

Sometimes skeptical non-believers assume that the presence of dinosaurs somehow invalidates the Bible. In fact, the word "dinosaur" was only coined within the last two centuries. It was first used by Dr. Richard Owens in 1841 when archeologists began to uncover evidence for these large prehistoric creatures. They thought they were finding something new, but the Bible had already recorded the existence of these two majestic creatures 4,000 years earlier!

Don't miss the point: it's not about Jurassic Park—it's about Jehovah's power. The only reason God noted these creatures was to demonstrate that if He could create such mysterious, powerful animals, He can do anything. He emphasized His point in Job 41:11–10 when He said, *"Who then is able to stand against me? Everything under heaven belongs to me."*

Have you come to a point in your life where you believe that God has unlimited power in every circumstance? You may think your situation is impossible, but God specializes in the impossible. When Gabriel told young Mary that she would give birth to the Messiah, she questioned him because she was a virgin. It was not possible for her to be pregnant. I love Gabriel's reply. He said, *"Nothing is impossible with God"* (Luke 1:37) In the midst of your impossible circumstances, hang on to these five powerful words: nothing is impossible with God!

Admit Your Inability to Understand God
When you've run out of answers, you can also do as Job did and admit your inability to understand God. There's a certain peace that comes with that admission. Job 42:3 says, *"I spoke things I did not understand, things too wonderful for me to know."* We all have a tendency to make people think we know more than we really do. However, like Job, we need to know that it's fine to admit that there are things beyond our understanding. I recall one Peanuts comic strip in which Lucy was dispensing psychiatric advice to Charlie Brown. She said, "Life is like a deck chair on a ship. Some place their chair so they can see where they've been, and others place it so they can see where they're going." To which Charlie Brown muttered, "And I can't even get mine unfolded!"

Job admitted to God that he didn't have everything figured

out. I sometimes laugh at some of the TV evangelists who preach that if you are right with God you will always enjoy health, wealth, and prosperity. Their message is, "God loves you and has a wonderful Porsche for your life." Their theology doesn't allow any room for righteous suffering. Yet those who have walked with God for the longest times and in the deepest fellowship recognize that there is a mystery about suffering that we will never understand.

A few days after the Islamic warriors attacked our nation on 9/11, Billy Graham spoke at a worship service held at the National Cathedral to provide some words of comfort and perhaps ascribe some meaning to what had happened. He said, "I have been asked hundreds of times in my life why God allows tragedy and suffering. I have to confess that I really do not know the answer totally, even to my own satisfaction. I have to accept, by faith, that God is sovereign, and He's a God of love and mercy and compassion in the midst of suffering."

Seek God's Face Instead of His Answers
What else can you do when life does not make sense? Job had run out of answers, but He discovered something better than answers when He found God. In Job 42:5 he said, *"My ears had heard of You, but now my eyes have seen You."* One advertising slogan for Radio Shack is: "You've got questions. We've got answers." Job's position was just the opposite. He said, "God, you've got questions, but I don't have any answers." People are still trying to find answers to the tough questions of life. However, Job discovered that it is better to seek God's face than to find answers.

Years ago, there was a television series called "All in the Family." Archie Bunker was the stereotypical, bigoted male chauvinist. His wife, Edith Bunker, was portrayed as a dingy, overly submissive wife. However, there was a verbal exchange in one episode where Edith said something profound.

Archie's son-in-law asked, "Tell me, Archie, if there is a God, why is this world messed up?" Archie rolls his eyes and says, "Why do I always have to give the answers? Edith, tell this dumb Polack why, if God created the world, it's in such a mess?" Edith thought for a moment and said, "Well, I suppose it's to make us appreciate heaven better when we get there." Edith was no dingbat—that's an astute observation about suffering. Life is full of pain and sorrow. That's one of the reasons why we're going to enjoy heaven so much!

Which one are you spending all your energy doing: seeking answers, or are you seeking God's face? At the beginning of Job's story, we learn that Job was already a very religious man. In Job 1:5, we read that Job made burnt offerings to God on behalf of his children. How did he know that God wanted him to offer sacrifices? Apparently, he had heard from some source that this was the way to relate to God. In other words, Job had *heard* about God, but it was not until he endured painful trials that he actually came *face to face* with God.

Before, he had what you might call an empty religion, and when he encountered God, he gained an eternal relationship with God. Which do you have? Have you just heard about religion from your parents, or your pastor, or from someone else? I don't really like religion. Religion is our attempt to try to appease God. Christianity is God reaching out to us to initiate a personal relationship.

There's an eternity of difference between religion (hearing about God) and a relationship (encountering God). Religion is like reading about a foreign country in a travel guide; a relationship is like visiting that country and experiencing it firsthand. Religion is like reading a recipe for delicious food; a relationship is like sitting down to enjoy the meal. Religion is like reading a newspaper ad for a convertible sports car; a relationship is like driving it with the wind blowing in your hair. Religion would be like watching the Masters Golf Tournament on television; a relationship is like teeing it up with Tiger Woods and actually playing a round of golf at Augusta!

Humble Yourself and Repent

In Job 42:6 Job says, *"I despise myself and repent in dust and ashes."* Before you can seek God's face, you must be willing to humble yourself and repent. In 2 Chronicles 7:14 God said, *"If my people, who are called by my name, will humble themselves and pray and seek my face and turn from their wicked ways, then will I hear from heaven and will forgive their sin and will heal their land."*

Job wasn't degrading himself when he said, "I despise myself." He was simply stating his condition as he stood before a perfect, holy God. His humble attitude reflected what Jesus said in Matthew 5:3, *"Blessed are the poor in spirit, for theirs is the kingdom of heaven."* Job admitted that he was spiritually bankrupt before God. Humility is not thinking lowly of yourself; it is not thinking of yourself at all. When you see God in all of His brilliant holiness, you will also see yourself in all of your sinful depravity. When Isaiah saw God high and lifted up, his response was, *"Woe is me, for I am a man of unclean lips"* (Isaiah 6:5).

When Job saw God, he fell on his face to repent of his sins. What sin? Job's mistake wasn't a brazen sin of the flesh. Job proved Satan wrong because he never cursed God to His face. Nevertheless, Job was guilty of trying to justify himself, and he was guilty of bitterness toward God. Do you know the best thing to do when you're going through a trial? Repent. You may argue, "Well, I don't know anything I've done that I need to repent of." Just get on your knees before God and ask Him to reveal any hidden, secret sins—and see what happens.

Why Do the Righteous Suffer?

Why good people suffer has remained a mystery throughout all generations. There are plenty of descendants of Job's friends who still believe that bad things happen to bad people. Even in the time of Jesus, people interpreted personal tragedy as God's punishment. One time, Jesus made reference to a couple of tragic events in which Jews were killed.

133

If there had been a Jewish 24-hour cable news network during the time of Jesus, these two events would have been the lead stories. I imagine it would have gone something like this:

> "Good evening, I'm Josephus Jeremias and this is the Lox News network. We have some breaking news. Governor Pontius Pilate ordered a detachment of Roman soldiers into the Temple today to break up the protests of the Galilean rebels. The rebels refused to leave, so swords were drawn. We have reports that several of the rebels were killed, and their blood was splattered near the altar of sacrifice. More details at eleven. In another unrelated story, eighteen Jewish construction workers were killed when the stone tower they were building at Siloam collapsed. The names of the deceased are being withheld pending notification of family members."

> Josephus turns to the camera and says, "And now to comment on these two breaking stories is Rabbi Hallel Ben Ezra. Rabbi, what's your take on these two events—one a man-made tragedy, and the other an unfortunate accident?"

> "Shalom, Josephus. These were not accidents. The truth is simple: The Galilean rebels got what was coming to them. They were blatant sinners and God was punishing them. The same can be said for the vile construction workers at the tower. Obviously, they were rotten to the core, too. That's why God caused the tower to fall and kill them."

> Josephus continues, "And now to be fair and balanced, we have a remote hook up with the roving Galilean teacher, Jesus of Nazareth. Jesus, are you there? Jesus, it's Josephus Jeremias here with Lox News…what do you have to say about these two terrible tragedies?

> Jesus answered, "Do you think that these Galileans were worse sinners than all the other Galileans because they suffered this way? I tell you, no! But unless you repent, you too will all perish. Or those eighteen who died when the tower in Siloam fell on them—do you think they were more guilty than all the others living in Jerusalem? I tell you, no! But unless you repent, you too will all perish" (Luke 13:1–5).

Jesus stressed that it is futile to try to figure out why bad things happen to people. He moved the issue beyond why and focused on what every one of us must do: repent! The word "repent" (*metanoia*) means: "a change of mind that leads to a change of behavior." In order to become a Christian, you must repent of your sins. Instead of thinking that your sins are just minor flaws that everybody does, you must change your mind. No sin is insignificant. Each sin is like spitting in the face of God or pounding the nails into the flesh of Jesus.

Even after you become a Christian, you must keep on repenting. Whenever you find that your thinking and God's thinking don't match, it's time to change your mind again. Job changed his mind and repented of the way he had been thinking about God. He made a mistake thinking that God was mean, vicious, and cruel. He crossed the line when he wanted to argue his case before God. However, once Job heard God's voice, and saw His face, Job realized that his thinking was all wrong.

Better Than Answers

No, Job didn't get the answers he was looking for—he got something much more valuable. He came to know God on a personal level. What do you do when you run out of answers? First, remind yourself that God is able to work in your behalf. He can do anything. Next, admit that there are questions in this life that will never be answered to your satisfaction. That means humbling yourself and realizing that God's ways are not your own. Finally, be open to discovering something *much better* than answers. That's Jesus—the Answer when answers aren't enough. When you make that precious discovery, you will find yourself at one of life's crucial turning points, which is where we next see Job in the climactic conclusion of his story. What we learn next from Job at this final, crucial point in the story will make all the difference in our ability to find peace in our pain.

"Character cannot be developed in ease and quiet. Only through experience of trial and suffering can the soul be strengthened, vision cleared, ambition inspired, and success achieved."

–Helen Keller

CHAPTER 13

Life's
Turning Points

❧❦

Have you ever heard the expression, "What you don't know can't hurt you?" That's not always the case. It reminds me of the funny story about a man who walked into a drug store and asked the pharmacist, "Do you have anything to cure hiccups?" The pharmacist said, "Look on aisle three." While the man was looking, the pharmacist snuck up behind him and screamed, "Boo!" and knocked the guy's legs out from under him. The dazed customer looked up from the floor and said, "What'd you do that for?" The pharmacist said proudly, "I'll bet you don't have the hiccups any more." The guy rubbed a knot on his head and said, "I never did. It's my wife out in the car who has them!" What you don't know *can* hurt you.

As we've examined the amazing story of Job, we must remember Job never knew that he was the subject of a heavenly test. What a difference it would have made if he had only known that his suffering was the result of a cosmic conversation between God and the adversary. If he'd only known that God wanted to show Satan that Job would *not* curse Him to His face. What a turning point that revelation would have been in Job's story.

Life is full of turning points. A turning point is a change of direction that leads to a change in destiny. For instance, the D-Day invasion of Normandy was a turning point in WWII that altered the course of history. We've all had personal turning points as well. When you graduate from school or take a new job, you come to a turning point. Life is never the same afterwards. Let's review what we've learned about finding peace in our pain by describing Job's four turning points.

1. Job Changed His Mind

The first turning point that Job experienced was when he repented. After God spoke to Job out of the storm, Job ran out of arguments. He changed his mind about who God was and how God was dealing with him. Notice, too, that when Job repented, he was still in the middle of his suffering. His grief over the death of his children still tore at his heart. Painful sores still covered his body. In other words, it's easier to change your attitude than your circumstances. Sometimes we have little or no control over our painful circumstances. The only thing you have power to change is your perspective on your unpleasant situation.

The Apostle Paul was a convict in prison when he wrote these powerful words: *"I have learned the secret of being content in any and every situation, whether well fed or hungry, whether living in plenty or in want. I can do all things through him who gives me strength"* (Philippians 4:12–13). Our natural response to suffering is to complain against God and try to change our circumstances. What was Paul's secret? Attitude. Changing your attitude in the midst of pain is learned behavior—it isn't instinctive. Suffering can either make you bitter or it can make you better—it's your choice.

Ted Turner is a millionaire media mogul who launched the first 24-hour cable news channel. He grew up in a religious family and even once considered being a missionary. However, all that changed when his younger sister, Mary Jane, contracted lupus and died. Reflecting on her death, Ted Turner said: "I was taught that God was love, and God was powerful. I couldn't understand how someone so innocent should be made or allowed to suffer so…if that's the kind of God he is, I want nothing to do with him."[16] How tragic! His ordeal with his sister turned him away from God instead of towards Him.

140

Ted Turner has many millions of dollars, but he doesn't have the one thing that matters—faith. Jesus said, *"What shall it profit a man if he gains the whole world, and loses his soul?"* (Mark 8:36).

In contrast, consider one of my spiritual heroes, George Mueller. In the 1800s, Pastor Mueller operated an orphanage in Britain. He cared for over 30,000 orphans and never once asked for financial support. God always supplied his needs because he was a great man of faith. Like Ted, George lost someone he loved, too. In 1870, his wife Mary contracted an illness and died after months of suffering. George spoke at her funeral, but notice the contrast between George Mueller and Ted Turner's attitude. George said, "I miss her in numberless ways, and shall miss her yet more and more. But as a child of God, and as a servant of the Lord Jesus, I bow. I am satisfied with the will of my Heavenly Father. I kiss continually the hand that has thus afflicted me."[17]

As you face pain and adversity, is your response closer to Ted Turner's or George Mueller's? Job repented *before* his circumstances changed. Remember this life-altering lesson: you can change your attitude easier than you can change your circumstances.

2. Job Stopped Defending Himself

After Job suffered the loss of all things precious, three "friends" came to comfort him. However, as Job described them, they were "miserable comforters." Their conclusion seemed logical enough. (1) The wicked suffer and the righteous prosper. (2) Job was obviously suffering. (3) Therefore, Job was a wicked man. Logic may be faultless, but if the premise is wrong, the conclusion will always be wrong. God rebuked these three theological stooges because they were wrong about God, and they were wrong about Job. In reality, Job wasn't suffering because he was the *worst* of men. He was suffering because he was the *best* of men! Four times in this passage God calls Job, "my servant."

141

Job's second turning point came when he finally gave up trying to defend himself against their onslaught of accusations. At that moment, God vindicated Job before his friends in Job 42:7–8:

> *After the Lord had said these things to Job, he said to Eliphaz the Temanite, "I am angry with you and your two friends, because you have not spoken of me what is right, as my servant Job has. So now take seven rams and go to my servant Job and sacrifice a burnt offering for yourselves. My servant Job will pray for you, and I will accept his prayer* (KJV: "him will I accept") *and not deal with you according to your folly. You have not spoken of me what is right, as my servant Job has."*

Satan has many tools at his disposal—including sincere people with false concepts about God. Satan even used Job's wife, who counseled Job to "curse God and die." Job's friends and his wife were sincere in their beliefs, but they were sincerely wrong.

When you're God's servant, He is your Defender. You don't need to defend yourself. The Psalmist declared, *"Let all those rejoice who put their trust in you, let them ever shout for joy, because You defend them...God is a father to the fatherless, a defender of widows..."* (Psalm 5:11; 68:5). There is only one kind of person God defends—the defenseless. For much of this story, Job had been arguing with his friends, defending himself. While he was busy doing that, God wouldn't defend him. Finally, Job gave up. He stopped talking and started repenting. That's when God stepped up and began to defend him. Do you want God to be your Defender? Then forfeit all your rights to Him.

3. Job Prayed for His Friends

The third turning point in Job's life was when he began to intercede for his three friends. God instructed them to go to Job and make a burnt offering in his presence. This was Job's final test. Would Job vent his hostility and resentment for these three men who had slandered him? Or would he accept the terms of God's treaty, embrace them, and forgive them? This would have been the perfect occasion for Job to gloat and say, "See, I told you! You were wrong, and I was right!" Instead of extracting revenge, Job simply did what God commanded. He accepted his friends and prayed for them.

Job 42:9–10 says, *"So Eliphaz the Temanite, Bildad the Shuhite and Zophar the Naamathite did what the Lord told them; and the Lord accepted Job's prayer. After Job prayed for his friends, the Lord made him prosperous again* (KJV: "turned his captivity") *and gave him twice as much as he had before."* To me, the most important word in that passage is the word "after." When Job prayed for his friends, he was still in agony. It wasn't until *after* he interceded for them that God reversed his situation. Job had experienced God's grace and forgiveness, so he was willing to extend the same generosity to his friends.

Many people think prayer is manipulating God to do something that otherwise He wouldn't do. Like rubbing Aladdin's lamp, we want God to appear and say, "Your wish is my command." *However, prayer is not getting God to do what we want—it is God getting us in a position to do what He wants.* One of the things He wants all of us to do is to forgive those who have hurt us.

You are enslaved until you can pray for those who have hurt you. Jesus said it this way, *"Bless those who curse you, pray for those who mistreat you"* (Luke 6:28). I like the King James Version that says, "God turned Job's captivity." What captivity? Job was enslaved to his own attitude of bitterness and unforgiveness. Praying for them indicated that he was willing to forgive these three men, just as God had forgiven him. The most common Hebrew word for "forgive" is *salach,* which means "to release." When you forgive others, you release them from the grip of your grudge. In the process of releasing them, you surrender your desire for revenge. When you forgive, *you* are the one who escapes the bondage of bitterness.

In one of my earlier books, *Handling Life's Disappointments*, I have a chapter on anger entitled, "When You Reach the Boiling Point." In it, I quote from Dr. S. I. McMillan: "The moment I start hating a man, I become his slave. I can't even do my work anymore because he even controls my thoughts. The man I hate hounds me. I cannot escape his tyrannical grasp on my mind. The person I resent may be miles from my bedroom, but more cruel than any slave driver, he whips my thoughts into such a frenzy that even my inner spring mattress becomes a rack of torture."[18]

The cause of your emotional pain may be because someone in your past injured you deeply and you are harboring resentment. Have you tried praying for him or her? Talk to God about that person and acknowledge that you must be willing to forgive. Do yourself a favor: forgive your enemies and start praying for them. It could be an enormous turning point in your life.

Have you noticed that there were specific things that Job did to trigger each of his turning points so far? For example, when he repented, then God vindicated him. When he prayed for his tormentors, then God rewarded his faithfulness. Is there something you need to repent of today? Are there people that you need to pray for and forgive? Take a step in that direction and you will release a chain reaction of blessing.

4. God Restored Job's Life

The final turning point in Job's story occurred when God restored what Job had lost. In fact, God gave Job more than he ever had before. Job 42:11–17 says, "*All his brothers and sisters and everyone who had known him before came and ate with him in his house. They comforted and consoled him over all the trouble the Lord had brought upon him, and each one gave him a piece of silver and a gold ring. The Lord blessed*

144

the later part of Job's life more than the first. He had fourteen thousand sheep, six thousand camels, a thousand yoke of oxen and a thousand donkeys. And he also had seven sons and three daughters. The first daughter he named Jemimah (her name means "Dove"), *the second Keziah* (which means cinnamon), *and the third Keren-Happuch* (which means "dark-eyes"). *Nowhere in all the land were there found women as beautiful as Job's daughters, and their father granted them an inheritance along with their brothers. After this Job lived a hundred and forty years; he saw his children and their children to the fourth generation. And so he died, old and full of years."* In His restoration of Job, God gave Job three specific blessings.

God Doubled His Wealth

After Job repented and prayed for his friends, things changed. He ended up with exactly twice as much livestock as before. In the first chapter of Job, we recall that he had 7,000 sheep, and in the end he had 14,000 sheep. He lost 3,000 camels, and in Chapter 42 we see he has 6,000 camels. He first had 500 yoke of oxen (two per yoke = 1,000 oxen). He ended up with 2,000 head of oxen. He started out with 500 donkeys, and in the end he had 1,000 donkeys.

If you wonder where he got his newfound wealth, notice that it says that Job's brothers, sisters, and other people came to support him. They had heard that Job had lost everything, so they all pitched in to help. God could have simply opened heaven to deliver livestock or money to Job, but He used these people to restore Job's wealth. Each of them brought Job a piece of silver and a gold ring. No doubt, this outpouring of generosity provided the venture capital for Job's financial recovery. Likewise, when you serve God, don't ever be surprised if He chooses to use other people to bless you.

God Doubled His Children

If you recall, Job had seven sons and three daughters in the first chapter. If God doubled his wealth, why didn't God give him 20 children? Did God let him down? Certainly not. Job still had 10 children in heaven, and now he had 10 children on earth—a *total* of 20 children. Today, he is with those children in heaven.

This should be a great comfort to any of you who have ever had the painful experience of burying a child. In 2 Samuel 12, King David had a newborn son who was critically ill. David prostrated himself on the ground praying and fasting for the child to recover. After a week, the child died. Afterward, David got up, cleaned his face, and went to the House of God to worship. Some of his servants questioned his behavior. They said, "While the child was alive, you fasted and wept, but now that the child is dead, you get up and eat!" David's response is one of the most powerful statements in the Bible about life after death. David said, *"While the child was still alive I fasted and wept. I thought, 'Who knows? The Lord may be gracious to me and let the child live.' But now that he is dead, why should I fast? Can I bring him back again? I will go to him, but he will not return to me"* (2 Samuel 12:22–23).

If you've ever buried a child, I hope you will realize that you didn't *lose* that child. You know where he or she is. That child cannot return to you, but if you are a servant of Jesus, you can go to him or her. I recall years ago after I shared this truth at my church, a couple approached me with tearful smiles and told me that exactly one year earlier their child had died. Learning this comforting truth from Job was a turning point in their grief. I have another friend who buried a child and told me, "I really have three children—two teenagers on earth and one child in heaven. Frankly, I worry sometimes about the two kids on earth, but I never worry a second about the one in heaven."

God Added Life to His Years
In our fitness-crazed culture, people are looking for special diets, exercise, and medicine to add years to their lives. God offers something far better. He can add *life* to your years! We

read of Job, *"The Lord blessed the latter part of Job's life more than the first...he died old and full of years"* (Job 42:12, 17). The phrase doesn't mean Job died as an old man; it means that he lived a full life. Job's true wealth was measured in terms of his family. He lived long enough to see his grandchildren, his great-grandchildren, and his great-great-grandchildren. The older we get, the more we understand that the greatest gifts we have are our relationships. You want to know how wealthy you are? Consider everything you have that money can't buy (and death can't take away) and you'll discover how rich you really are.

Saving the Best for Last

People often speak of the patience of Job, but patience is a passive emotion. What Job really had was perseverance—and that's an active conviction. The New Testament gives us the last word on Job in James 5:11: *"We consider blessed those who have persevered. You have heard of Job's perseverance and have seen what the Lord finally brought about. The Lord is full of compassion and mercy."* Wouldn't it have been sad if the book of Job ended with Chapter 41 when Job was still miserable, weak, and poor? However, Job didn't quit. He persevered and experienced all the blessings we read in Chapter 42 as a reward for his faithfulness.

Take a look at your life's circumstances right now. You may be in Job 41 where things are dark and bleak and you don't have any answers to your problems. Don't quit. Don't give up on God. Remember what happened in the next chapter in Job's life and all the blessings he received because of his perseverance. Your turning points are just ahead—so put on your blinker!

That's the thing about God—He always saves the best for last! Do you recall the first public miracle of Jesus? It was at a wedding party in Cana where Jesus was a guest. They had run out of wine, which was a terrible breach of hospitality. Jesus' mother asked Him to do something, so Jesus quietly changed water into wine. When the guest of honor tasted this new wine, he made this observation to the groom, *"Everyone else begins with the choice wine, and then when everyone is full, he brings out the cheap stuff. But you have saved the best for last"* (John 2:10).

That's the difference between Jesus and the devil. The devil always serves his best first, and then it gets progressively worse. The prodigal son started out with wine, women, and song, but he ended up with pigs, slop, and filth. Millions of people are constantly searching for peace in life through the next pill, the next snort, or the next on-the-edge experience. The world, the flesh, and the devil always operate according to the law of diminishing returns. What starts as a moment of pleasure always ends up as an eternity of misery. You won't find peace there.

However, Jesus always saves the best for last. If you are a follower of Jesus Christ, you can find peace in the midst of whatever pain you're going through now because you know that the best years of your life are always ahead of you. The best may come after you die, but it *will* come. For a person who rejects Jesus, *this* life is as good as it will ever get. Those who serve and love Jesus are the only ones who really do live happily ever after.

ENDNOTES

CHAPTER 2
1. Commentary on Job, Dr. J. Vernon McGee, p. 16.
2. The Writings of George Washington, ed. John C. Fitzpatrick (Washington: United States Government Printing Office, 1931-44), vol. 30, pp. 292-296.
3. Don't Waste Your Sorrows, Paul Billheimer, p. 102.

CHAPTER 3
4. Mere Christianity, C.S. Lewis, p. 190.
5. Tracks of a Fellow Struggler, John Claypool, pp. 63-64.

CHAPTER 4
6. According to dictionary.com

CHAPTER 5
7. Postmodern Pilgrims, Leonard Sweet.
8. When I Was Diagnosed with Cancer, Linda Mae Richardson.
9. God's Outrageous Claims, Lee Stroble.

CHAPTER 7
10. According to dictionary.com
11. Parade Magazine, April 2008.
12. Mere Christianity, C.S. Lewis, chapter on God in the Dock, p. 160.
13. Mere Christianity, C.S. Lewis, p. 55.

CHAPTER 8
14. Systematic Theology, Paul Tillich, p. 414.

CHAPTER 10
15. The Problem of Pain, C.S. Lewis, Chapter 6.

CHAPTER 13
16. "Meet Ted Turner," Readers Digest, September, 1998.
17. George Mueller of Bristol, A.T. Pierson, p.161.
18. None of These Diseases, S.I. McMillan, p. 72.

Printed in the United States
211652BV00004B/1/P

9 780615 260082